# YOU WRITE THE TICKET, LORD

by
**Dorothy A. Galde**

**Here's Life Publishers, Inc.**

**San Bernardino, California 92402**

**YOU WRITE THE TICKET, LORD**
By Dorothy A. Galde

Published by
HERE'S LIFE PUBLISHERS, INC.
P.O. Box 1576
San Bernardino, CA 92402

Library of Congress Catalog Card 83-047516
ISBN 0-89840-047-3
HLP Product No. 950535
©1983, Here's Life Publishers, Inc.

The poems, "Grace to Grace" and "The Music of My Life," by Neva Thompson, ©1975, are used by permission.

Lyrics to the song, "Through It All," by Andrae Crouch, ©1971 by Manna Music, Inc., are used by permission.

Scripture quotations are from the King James Version of the Bible.

# CONTENTS

Preface . . . . . . . . . . . . . . . . . . . . . . . . . . . . . . 9

Acknowledgments . . . . . . . . . . . . . . . . . . . . . 11

Foreword . . . . . . . . . . . . . . . . . . . . . . . . . . . 13

## PART I
### THE SOWING: Romans 8:28 Contemplated

The Music of My Life . . . . . . . . . . . . . . . . . . . . . 16

1. Two Commitments . . . . . . . . . . . . . . . . . . . . 17

2. Journey to Happiness . . . . . . . . . . . . . . . . . . 25

3. Thanksgiving and Heartbreak . . . . . . . . . . . . . 37

## PART II
### THE GROWING: Romans 8:28 Examined

From Grace to Grace . . . . . . . . . . . . . . . . . . . . 54

4. Struggle . . . . . . . . . . . . . . . . . . . . . . . . . . . . . 55

5. New Hope, New Happiness . . . . . . . . . . . . . . 61

6. Disaster . . . . . . . . . . . . . . . . . . . . . . . . . . . . . 77

7.  Rebuilding . . . . . . . . . . . . . . . . . . . . . . . . . . . . . 93

8.  The Fire . . . . . . . . . . . . . . . . . . . . . . . . . . . . . 111

**PART III**

THE REAPING: Romans 8:28 Trusted

Through It All . . . . . . . . . . . . . . . . . . . . . . . . . . . . 128

9.  Memory Stones . . . . . . . . . . . . . . . . . . . . . . 129

10.  Four-Point Plan . . . . . . . . . . . . . . . . . . . . . 139

**NOTES** . . . . . . . . . . . . . . . . . . . . . . . . . . . . . 147

*To those who hurt,*
*with love and*
*understanding.*

# PREFACE

*Kites rise against the wind.*
   *So do airplanes.*
      *So do people.*
*Dr. V. R. Edman, President of Wheaton College*
   *Said to me years ago,*
      *"Dottie,*
*you have to write a book*
   *to let others know of the*
      *bouquet of difficulties*
*the Lord has been pleased to present you.*
   *There are books we can give*
      *to those who have suffered physically,*
*to those who have lost a loved one,*
   *but He has given you such a*
      *garland of griefs*
*you must share it."*
   *I wrote and rewrote,*
      *I submitted and submitted,*
*I waited and waited.*
   *But God has His own time,*
      *and it is perfect.*
*My desire is that others may be encouraged,*
   *and that Christ may be lifted up.*

*Dorothy A. Galde*
*Prescott, Arizona 1982*

# ACKNOWLEDGMENTS

*To my husband Lloyd for his care of me and of our home and for his complete support, all of which has made my life appetizing.*

*To our children, Pete, Dan, Ted and Suzy for being challenges in the past and now mainstays — physically, emotionally and spiritually.*

*To Georgiana Walker for her expertise, her concern, her assistance and her prayers.*

*To friends all over the country who have asked for this story in print.*

# FOREWORD

*You Write the Ticket, Lord is the gripping story of one family's experience of Romans 8:28, possible only when planned by an omniscient, gracious, loving God. No conscientious writer of fiction could match the chapter-by-chapter events which befell this one who sincerely wanted the will of God in her life.*

*This is the kind of book you will not want to put down until you have read it from cover to cover. Having known the major participants since college days, I can affirm that this is not a set of pat answers for those in suffering, nor is the account glorified by exaggeration of its heart-throbbing incidents. The story is told as it really was, with all the heartaches, joys, sorrows, and struggles that somehow were packed into the life of the author and her family.*

*If there is any question as to whether Romans 8:28 really can be fulfilled in someone's life, this book will provide the answer. All those who have deep and abiding hurts will be encouraged when they see how one person's faith triumphed in what, to an unbelieving soul, would seem to be a kaleidoscope of incredible disasters.*

*Here is a book that will encourage your faith, fortify your soul for sorrows yet unknown, and enrich your life with the revelation of a God in whose omniscience and love you can rest secure.*

*John F. Walvoord*

# PART I

## THE SOWING: Romans 8:28
## Contemplated

*"Not that we are sufficient of ourselves to think any thing as of ourselves; but our sufficiency is of God," (2 Cor. 3:5).*

# The Music of My Life

You are the way, I praise You every day,
And once again on bended knee each night,
You are the music of my life.
There are those who've never heard the song.
Lord, they have been in darkness for so long.
They have yet to know the joy You bring
Guide me gently, Lord, that I may sing,
And I will sing a song of gentle praise:
Thank you, Lord for Your most loving ways.
I treasure all the love I ever knew
Which in the end was heaven-sent by You.
Stand with me beside the narrow gate;
Let me learn to serve You while I wait.
And all the while I shall not stand alone,
For I will have a song to carry home.
I sing the song of everlasting life
Echoing the harmony in Christ.
I will sing Your praise in all I do,
And in the end, the song comes back to You.
You are the way, I praise You every day,
And once again on bended knee each night
You are the music of my life.

© 1975   Neva Thompson

16

## Two Commitments

"We have just today received a cablegram with the information that John and Betty Stam were murdered in Manchuria a week ago by marauding soldiers." The sobered Wheaton College senior stood before the regular crowd at the Tuesday evening Student Prayer Meeting. It was 1932.

"Two years ago," the speaker went on, "John and Betty sat where you're sitting." I moved uncomfortably. "On a night like this," he said, "I remember their declaring, 'We don't know what Christ has called us to do, but we're going because we trust Him—with our lives. Whatever he has in store for us will be fine. We're not afraid'."

And *this* had happened. Roughly routed out of their beds, they were marched to the center of the village and forced to state that they were American spies. They were burned, cut, hosed, killed and dismembered.

*Impossible. This is a civilized world,* I thought. *Can such inhumanity exist?* John and Betty Stam's death proved it did.

They had gone with the love of Christ in their hearts to bring a light to the people of Manchuria. Now the Stams were dead. What a waste. And God had allowed it to happen. Why?

If great honor had come to them, we would have been glowing, praising God together, and moving on to the next piece of business. But, as

C.S. Lewis points out, "God whispers to us in our pleasures, speaks in our conscience, but shouts in our pains: it is His megaphone to rouse a deaf world."

"How many of you are willing to lay your lives on the line for Christ?" the speaker asked. "Are you ready, are you able to say—with *no* idea of what the Lord has in store for you—'Thy will be done. No holds barred.'? Can you give up *your* blueprint for life and let Him pull His blueprint out and set it in motion? Bear in mind what this could cost."

Silence of a different kind pervaded the room— a silence of searching, deep thought. Commitment. No one felt the need to rise and shine in this renunciation of self; it was a private matter between each person and the Lord. Finally the quiet was broken by several prayers. A subdued crowd went out into the cold, starlit night.

God broke my heart that night.

As much as I loved life, my kind of life—the fun kind—I had to meet that challenge. All that evening I wrestled, rationalized, excused myself from taking that route. Yet, I couldn't put it down. God wouldn't let me.

I went to the college newspaper office with some of the others who worked on the *Record*. They chided me for my lack of participation in the usual muted racket that filled the office. The hush from prayer meeting had worn off for them. It was business as usual, but not for me.

The news article I was writing had to be finished by morning, but it had lost its importance. I completed it after a fashion and moved over to an empty typewriter to finalize the copy.

A tall blond Norwegian named Donovan Penheiter, immediate past editor of the *Record,* walked into the office. A big-man-on-campus, Don was in his senior year of pre-med. As a sophomore, I was in awe of him.

He came over to me. "May I take you home when you're through?" he asked.

Our blue eyes met. I hesitated and then answered, "Yes, if you don't mind my bouncing some heavy stuff on you. I'm not in a cheerful mood."

"Ditto for me. Nobody's very bubbly this evening. John was a good friend. . . makes you want to pick up the torch, or something," he finished lamely.

After I turned my article in, we walked down the path between the elms without saying much. It was hard to know where to start. Don was carrying my books. He broke the silence. "Death is not new to me. My father died of a coronary thrombosis when I was nine. My sister Eunice died of a pulmonary thrombosis during my freshman year. Same cause. We all had the flu right after the war in 1919."

I could see from his face that his sister had been more than special.

"Accepting my father's death and Eunice's has been the most difficult exercise of my faith in Christ. My mother is a giant in the faith-rest

department. I'm not. Not yet." He spoke of his
mother with tenderness.

"Are you as afraid as I am to turn your whole
life over to the Lord? That's what I wanted to talk
about. It's so hard, and yet I think I have to do it,"
I said.

"Not afraid. Not really. He accomplishes His
plans whether we give Him permission or not, I
find. I wish I could look ahead and get some idea
of what His plans entail. Maybe I'd be more willing then."

I spoke up quickly, maybe too quickly, "Oh, I'm
on the other end of the stick. I don't want to know.
I want to say *yes* in blind faith. I don't think I care
what God wants of me, but I want to *know* I can
trust Him with my life. That's an awful thing to say,
I guess."

"In some ways, maybe it is, but don't we all
have the same nagging fear that if we say, 'Go to
it, Lord, whatever You want,' He'll say, 'Aha! I've
got you in my power!' and then the blows will begin
to fall." Don had hit the nail on the head.

I was using him as a sounding board. After all,
he was two years older than I and had lived
through more traumatic experiences. I had lost my
mother when I was two, but my father married
again when I was four, and I dearly loved the only
mother I had ever known.

"If I were to say, 'Okay, You write the ticket,
Lord' what would change? Can't God in His
sovereignty and omnipotence cause anything He
wants anyway—no matter what I say?" I asked.

"Technically, yes, He can; but I don't think He does. We're leaving out the fact that God's reason for allowing difficult experiences usually is to bring us closer to Him. That comes from His love, not from glee that He has you in His power." He paused, and then went on, "You know what you're doing, don't you? You're making me back down on my major premise. You're making me think through the rubbish that has cluttered my thinking."

"If God's loving us through suffering brings us into closer relationship with Him, then it serves a good purpose." I was talking to myself as well as to Don.

"Romans 8:28: 'And we *know* that all things work together for good to them that love God, to them who are the called according to His purpose,' he quoted.

"My father's favorite verse," I said. "I've been brought up on that one. But did you find that the deaths of your father and sister really did work together for good?"

"Not yet, but somewhat against my will, I have to admit that they can. I spent time hating God for denying what I thought was rightfully mine. In the end, I learned that He was the only one I could turn to. No one else understood, not even my mother. It was different for her."

An hour later as I snuggled under the warm covers of my bed, I turned toward the wall so my roommate wouldn't see me. I closed my eyes and said, "Father, I want You to know I'm yours for

better or for worse. Help me never to say no to You.
Take me, do with me what You will. Take from
me what comes between us. You write the ticket,
Lord. I trust You. I know I'll have to face this again
and again and say yes over and over, but I want
Your desire for my life more than anything else.
I love you."

Several weeks later I went home for Christmas.
Although I was 600 miles from Wheaton, Don sent
me two dozen long-stemmed red roses. The card
said, "You know what red roses mean."

It frightened me. I wasn't grown up enough for
*love*. My sister Lillian brought it into focus. "I love
you" was something I could handle, she pointed
out.

In fact, I was so willing to handle it, I went back
to Wheaton early. Don had spent the whole vacation on campus in the chem lab. I could put the
three extra days into study, I told myself.

One evening before school reconvened, Don
and I met Mal and Enid, his roommate and mine,
who were engaged, for a game of Rook at Don's
rooming house. Mal and Enid left early after the
men served refreshments, and Don and I sat on the
divan in front of the fire.

Don slid to the floor with his long legs stretched
out in front of him. Then he turned and searched
my face. "I know I have no right to ask you this.
I have four years of medical school and then in-
ternship, but tonight I found I don't want to look
ahead alone any longer. Will you wait for me? I
want you to be my wife."

Blood pounded in my ears. No voice. All that I knew of him, especially his Christ-centeredness, brought joy and peace to my heart.

"Yes. I'll wait. I'll wait for you as long as it takes," I finally said. I didn't see the waiting, only the end product.

An ice storm had embedded the world in crystal and we walked home together under the branches enclosed in glass. When the wind blew, the branches clacked like castinets. We clung together, muffling our laughter as we slipped and slid.

Two commitments, one to my Lord, and one to Donovan, would shape my future in countless, unknown ways.

CHAPTER
TWO

## Journey to Happiness

At Commencement time I met Don's mother. He called her "Moth." On the porch at Don's house, a tall stately woman rose to meet us as we proceeded up the walk.

"Dorothy," she said searching my face. "My dear, I have prayed for you since before you were born."

How does one respond to such news? I dove into her open arms. There was nothing to fear. She was a friend to be cherished.

Two years of separation stretched before us. Don would be taking the first half of his medical training at the University of North Dakota at Grand Forks. I would finish at Wheaton in two years. We wrote every day, but letters are a poor substitute.

The two years ground away with few exciting interludes. I thought many times, *It's so easy to say, "Anything, Lord," and it's so hard to live each lonely day as though it's part of the "anything."* I forgot that the pain of separation could be part of God's plan for me, for us. If it were a test God was engineering, I flunked and flunked.

From season to season through the two years, I watched with envy as other couples strolled between the autumn-garbed elms, frolicked in the powdery snow around The Tower, and wandered down iris-bordered paths.

In June of 1934, Don came for my graduation.

He had been absent during my three bouts on crutches with a badly sprained ankle, always the same one. He'd missed the black eye covering half my face, consequence of two heads cracking in basketball. My many-colored visage had steered people away from my table in the dining hall. Looking at it was hard on the appetite. How all these events fitted under the "all things" I couldn't quite figure out, but I tried.

When we were finally in each other's presence again, I felt confused. There was pain I hadn't counted on. My fantasies didn't coincide with reality. Misunderstanding took us away from a banquet early to walk the fragrant June evening in misery.

"But you said—"

"But that's not what I *meant*."

"I can't *believe* you! You're making a mountain out of nothing!"

"No, I'm not. You've got to *give* a little," and so it went. We walked home cold, miserable, disillusioned. It was going to take a while to find each other again.

Had God planned this, or was He just permitting it?

Fortunately, both of us knew how to say, "I'm sorry."

A summer together at my home in western New York was filled with painting the house, picking cherries, playing tennis, riding in the rumble seat on a date with my sister Lillian and her fiance, Paul. These were the kinds of "all things" I could easily see working together for good.

Don had been accepted at Northwestern Medical School in Chicago in the fall. We were in the middle of the Great Depression. Chicago schools were paying in script. Little chance of a job there. I took a job as waitress at Lawson YMCA receiving $7.00 every two weeks and two meals a day. Tips were non-existent; it was a cafeteria. My room at the Dearborn Hotel up the street cost $3.00 a week. I had one whole dollar to squander on stamps and toothpaste every two weeks.

Don waited tables for his evening meal and ran an elevator at Lawson Y in his free time. His mother paid the tuition at Northwestern. The world was groaning under extreme pressure, and we groaned with it. The girl who had sat next to me in chapel at Wheaton for four years became my roommate. After months at the Y, we found jobs as waitresses at the exclusive Women's University Club of Chicago in the Loop with the satisfying salary of $50.00 a month. Now I would have the money to begin making my trousseau.

The wedding day, August 28, 1935, brought Lillian and Paul Robinson together as husband and wife, and Donovan and me. Since Paul was studying for the ministry, Lillian said that I could be *well* for nothing, but she could be *good* for nothing.

A honeymoon on the Great Lakes steamer, *The City of Detroit*, brought all the separation, all the partings, the reams of letters to an end. That was over. Gone forever. After four years of waiting, the world was shut out. All of love was ours.

God's plan in our lives was good. The very

heartbreak of separation made the joy of union more glorious. I could take any amount of this kind of plan from God. It had been worth the wait. However, I found that there's always a comedown after the honeymoon.

Back to waitressing and the studying, life was not a bowl of any kind of fruit. Many nights I would come home with bleeding feet, but Don was there to doctor them. When he would come in smelling of ether, my stomach turned upside down. It would take practice to like that odor. One evening as Don rubbed my feet, I told him, "The cook threw a knife at me today."

"She *what?*" he barked.

"She threw a French knife at me. I saw it coming and stepped aside. It sailed into the wall beside me."

"You don't have to go back. You know that, don't you?"

"No. I don't know that. Where else can I make $50 a month? She'll never do it again. It scared her as much as it did me. The Lord's in charge. I didn't do anything to bring it on but give her four orders, as usual. She was in a bad mood. Don't worry. Please." I suffered less than Don did over that episode. I've found since that it is always easier to suffer than to see someone you love hurt.

Most of the big problems of learning to live together were settled in our first few months. But one continued to irritate me: Don's sneezing. When he awoke every morning of the world, he sneezed and sneezed and sneezed. It cut through my awaken-

ing haze like a machete. Knowing how difficult it
was for me made it doubly hard for him, because
he couldn't help it. One day he came with the
grand announcement that a nose and throat
specialist at school was going to do an ionization
operation. The polyps in his nose and the entire
mucous membrane inside his nasal passage would
be removed.

After the operation, two medical students half-
carried him up the stairs to the apartment. He
looked ghastly. His nose was filled with packing.
He refused morphine, whispering, "I don't want
that. I want to know how this feels all the way
through." They overruled, and it was several hours
before he awoke demanding his watch.

From then on, life was a lab experiment and
Don was the guinea pig. I had to note on paper
the times of inhalation and exhalation. I felt guil-
ty. I knew he wouldn't have undergone such an
operation if his morning sneezes hadn't undone me.
He had been given no assurance that the operation would work. We could only hope.

"Oh, Lord, give me more cushion," I prayed.

Shortly after Don returned to health, I sensed
uneasiness in him that was not typical. I had learned not to pry; he would tell me when he was ready.

One night he came in after an evening lecture.
It was late. He had been walking in the snow,
wrestling by himself. I was asleep when I felt him
kneeling by my side. "I've been accepted for intern-
ship in three places," he said. "Minneapolis,
Chiciago, and Duluth." My heart raced with joy.

Chicago! Then I remembered he had applied at St. Luke's in Duluth, not expecting an appointment. It was the one place he wanted because he would go into practice with his uncle in Bagley, Minnesota. It was the right choice, but it left me out. He had to take it. I knew he had to.

*Another year of separation*, I thought, and then the cushion I'd prayed for appeared. "It's only for a year," I said. "We'll have uncounted years, the rest of our lives to be together."

The next Sunday we went to Wheaton to see Dr. Wallace Emerson, dean of the college. He offered me a job in his office, and I accepted. That took care of me. By June I was moved to Wheaton, and Don was in Duluth.

"Come unto Me all ye that labor and are heavy laden, and I will give you rest...and ye shall find rest unto your souls. For My yoke is easy, and My burden is light."[1] *Light*, Lord? Who's kidding whom? I didn't know that the burden is light only when I let Him carry it. I hadn't learned that yet.

I gritted my teeth and said yes again to His will. There's no joy in doing it that way.

*All things.* Oh, brother!

Shafts of light relieved the darkness, and yet, it wasn't all dark. Dr. Kilby, Mrs. Smith, Dr. Emerson were wonderful to work for. With students all around I almost felt I was back in school.

I went to Duluth for the Christmas vacation. I felt like the feminine lead in a Dr. Kildare series. I could see Don every moment he wasn't actively engaged in the care of patients. We'd sit and read the paper or talk until "Calling Dr. Penheiter" moved him to the telephone to check out the summons. "Sit tight, Mrs. P.; Duluth is about to welcome another citizen," he'd say with a kiss before he swished out of the room. He looked like Dr. Kildare, six feet tall, blond, and slim.

The vacation was over too soon. *Six months, just six months more,* I thought, as I went back to Chicago on *The Empire Builder.* I leaned my head back on the hard cushion and closed my eyes. I was utterly weary of leaving Don, of always living in the future. Letter-writing was a chestnut. I was drained with pushing down my natural desires.

I supposed God was teaching me patience, but I wanted to learn it quickly. How could I know that the day would come when I would thank Him for these years of separation? That never entered my head as a possibility.

The interlude between Christmas and June passed swiftly—in retrospect. We met in Minneapolis and were on our way to Bagley the following day. Don knew this town of Bagley better than his own stethoscope. He'd listened to its heartbeat since childhood. His Uncle Leroy, his mother's brother, had been waiting for him for years.

Mary, his aunt, enclosed us both in an enveloping hug when we arrived at the apartment above the hospital. Her excitement kept her sputtering between the baked ham in the oven and the salad at the sink.

"Leroy's been checking in every hour hoping for the news. We didn't know when you were coming. You don't believe in sending telegrams or anything like that, do you?" She gave the phone a solid crank. "Hi, Nancy, let me talk to Leroy. The kids are here!" Her voice sang with happiness. "Leroy. They're here. You coming home now?"

"Tell him I'll walk down to meet him," Don broke in.

After he left, and I was setting the table, Mary said, "Oh, Dottie, you kids can't know what this day means to Leroy and me. He's been too busy for too long. He needs to rest. I hope he can in a few weeks when Don get the feel of the practice. You'll stay here with us for a while, won't you? there's nothing vacant now except a big old eight-room house over on the highway. You wouldn't want that."

I gulped. What we wanted more than any other thing in the world was a home of our own. Not many days passed before we were inspecting the "big old eight-room house on the highway." The kitchen was overpowered by a black dragon—a wood stove. I walked up to it. "Look, Buster," I addressed it personally, "Let's get this straight. If I come here, I'm the boss."

Don put his hand on my forehead. "There's a name for people who talk to the furniture."

We took the house. We'd be pioneers. It was quite a change from the apartment in Chicago. A pump on the kitchen sink brought the water, a pantry and root cellar completed the conveniences. There were 12 foot ceilings, windows to the floor, a big brown space heater in the corner of the living room for winter warmth, and a bathroom on the second floor—one of few in Bagley. The plaster was falling down, leaving ribs of lath exposed.

We corralled the Nordstrom brothers to replaster, although they were 'purty busy mosta th' time.' Since we'd paid the first month's rent, we moved in, plastering or no. We picked up a walnut bed and dresser at a second-hand store downtown, and an unpainted kitchen table and chairs.

The Nordstroms tore off the rest of the plaster the first day. Next morning at six they drove up and left before Don could get down to the door. A note was tied to the doorknob.

Dear Doc. We have a job in Fargo that we promised a coupla weeks ago. Have to go and do it. Be back in a coupla weeks. Hope you don't mind. Nordstrom.

I was close to tears. Why did these things have to happen? Don put his arm around me. "We don't really care that much, do we? It'll be fun to camp out here for a couple of weeks."

He was right. He always said, "It doesn't matter where you are. It's who you're with that counts."

Having the Lord and Don at the hub of my life, the spoke neatly fanned out toward a rim of contentment. I reached into the pocket of my mind and fingered over the words Daddy so often quoted: "All things work together for good to them that love God, to them who are the called according to His purpose."

*Happiness is on the inside,* I thought. *If anticipation is the first third of joy, I can't imagine how good the second and third third will be.*

As we were having supper one evening, the phone rang. "It's Mrs. Peterson. She's in labor," Don said as he kissed me and grabbed his coat. "It's not going to be an easy delivery. Don't wait up for me."

At 10:00 he called, "Honey, this is going to be an all-night stand. Convulsions. Leroy is 40 miles north on another O.B. See you at breakfast, I hope. I love you."

I'd heard of doctor's all-night calls for years. This was the first. It was fun. I wondered if I'd think that forty years down the road. I wasn't worried.

Some hours later I awoke suddenly with a sharp pain in my side. Appendicitis? No. Everybody always thought that. Aspirin didn't help. I waited until 7 A.M. before making my way downstairs to the telephone. Up all night, Don had just left the hopital and gone to Mary and Leroy's for a nap. At 8:00 I called their apartment. After I described my pain, Don and Leroy came right over. With the room half-filled with doctors, the pain stopped. I was furious. They left. I took a bath—why, I'm not sure. Nausea swept over me. Fortunately some of the cooking pans were upstairs. I found one in time.

Mary came to check on me at about eleven. She took one look and fled to the telephone. They operated within the hour.

It was 3 A.M. when I regained consciousness.

I started to turn over and gasped to multicolored pain. Don was beside me instantly.

"Oh, Honey, Honey," he breathed, "how could we have known it was so bad? Why didn't you tell us?"

"I hate sissies."

"It was gangrenous. It burst in Leroy's hand. Even he got the shakes."

"I feel as though a truck has run over my middle," I said sleepily. He faded away.

In the far distance I heard Don talking, "The Lord took my father, He took my sister, but if He'd taken you, it would have wiped out my faith."

Two weeks went by before Leroy said I could go home. Don burst into the room, "The guy who owns this joint is gone, and I plan to kidnap you *now*. He says I can work off the hospital bill in the kitchen, nights. He's all heart, that man."

What a wonderful feeling to be alive and going home! I didn't dare ask if the plasterers had finished.

The kitchen sparkled. The stove shone like black satin.

"Oh, Don! It's all done! How did you ever manage?"

"Not I! The neighbors did everything: papering, painting, unpacking. What have I forgotten?"

"Nothing! All we need now is furniture, rugs, and curtains."

"There are some people who are never satisfied. Wait," he said grinning, "I knew I'd forgotten something. Look in the pantry."

The shelves were loaded with homemade jelly, jam, pickle, canned fruit and vegetables, and a loaf of homemade bread and a jar of homemade butter.

"Half the town wanted to be in on the pounding party."

"Pounding party? What's that?"

"Everybody brings a pound or a pint of something," he explained. "They've been bringing things to the office for days. It's their way of letting us know they're glad we're here."

I shook my head. I never dreamed that "all things" could include *this*.

## Thanksgiving and Heartbreak

'I don't think you ever knew I was a bad risk—from an insurance standpoint, did you?" Don asked as we drove to Minneapolis on a beautiful fall day. We were going to buy furniture for the house.

'What do you mean?" I was puzzled.

"You know my father and Eunice both died of a thrombosis."

"Yes. But what does that have to do with your insurance?"

"I have the same medical history as theirs. I had W.W.I influenza too."

"Is that what the doctors thought caused their deaths?"

"Yes. It seemed to weaken the vascular system in its victims. Breaks in the vessels caused hemorrhaging; this formed a blood clot, a thrombosis. But there's no need for you to worry," he went on. "I used to, but Leroy gave me a routine physical last week at the request of my insurance company. Now I'll be a standard risk. I sent my policy back so they can remove the sub-standard rating."

I realized my relief, great as it was, still couldn't be as great as his. This sword of Damocles had hung over his head for eighteen years. But I was relieved. Everything was wonderful, wonderful in my world.

We chose rugs, lamps, tables, chairs, and a divan in one day. The furniture arrived on the Mon-

day before Thanksgiving. Don worked up an appetite for dinner Thursday morning by chopping up
the crates into stove wood.

We had invited an old friend of Don's for dinner. She was a widow with a 10-year-old boy. They
came early and Jimmy helped Don outdoors.
Nancy and I put the good china on the new
mahogany table. We'd never used it before. This
was my kind of playing house. We ate to the point
of discomfort.

The next night Leroy and Mary came over to
eat the venison steaks he'd sent home with Don.
Apple pie was cooling in the pantry.

While I was cutting the pie, Leroy's voice
boomed out. "That apomorphine now on the
market is supposed to be the best thing yet to in-
duce vomiting. Y'don't suppose this talk'll bother
Dorothy, do you?"

Don laughed. "That means more pie for us if
it does."

We talked until late. It was eleven when they
left.

The next morning I woke with a start. The
alarm clock had failed to function. Don was late.
He sped up the stairs to wash. I flapped into the
kitchen, still wrestling with one bedroom slipper.

Ten minutes later as I stirred the oatmeal, Don
stood in the doorway, dressed and ready for the
mastoidectomy he had scheduled for 8:30. He had
a funny look.

I turned to pump water into the oatmeal pan,
and out of the corner of my eye I saw him fall.

When I swung around, he was lying face down on the floor. He turned his head and spoke with effort, "Call Leroy."

I ran to the phone and cranked it a long turn. Nancy would be on duty now. "Operator," she said automatically.

"Nancy, this is Dottie. Get Leroy, *please.*"

I heard her clicking and fussing, then, "Dottie, I don't know what's wrong, but his line is dead. It's never happened before. They take special care of Doc's line. What's wrong?"

"It's Don. Something's wrong with him. I'll run down there. Thanks, though."

Those words had thawed through the frozen pit of my stomach. Just saying them. I had to dress and get to the hospital, fast. I turned and ran back to the kitchen. Don was dragging himself along the floor with his left arm. His right arm looked helpless.

"Help me," he whispered.

I put my arms under him and tried to lift him onto the divan. He was heavy. He wasn't helping. I scrambled to my feet to get better leverage.

He looked at me. His eyes! One was large, iris opened completely. The other iris was a pinprick. My mouth watered.

"I can't get Leroy," I said as I held the upper part of his body on the divan and lifted his legs. "I'll dress and run down there."

He struggled to speak, "Get paper. Must write Leroy."

"Oh, dear God, what's happening?" I said

aloud. Panic welled up in me. Panic and terror. Strangers, they had invaded my home.

Bringing paper and pencil, I knelt beside him. He wrote with his left hand. He was not lefthanded.

"Promise you won't read this," he whispered.

I nodded. I threw on clothes. Taking my heavy jacket out of the closet, I went back to him. He was struggling to fold the letter. I wanted to grab the paper, jam it into the envelope, and run. I wanted to scream. Didn't he know that time was precious?

Putting my cheek to his forehead, I took the letter and sped for the back door.

The cold bit my face. I ran across the highway. Pain knifed my ribs. "Oh, God, don't let Leroy be away," I pleaded.

He was shaving, quiet and composed as I burst into the upper hall. I shoved Don's letter at him. "He's sick. He fell in the kitchen. His eyes are funny, one big, one little. He wrote with his left hand. He can't use the other." I was crying now. "I tried to call. Your phone's out of order."

Leroy scarcely moved during the barrage of words. He shook his head, "It can't be. He's too young!" he said. As he raced to the bedroom, he called, "You go back, I'll be right there."

When I got back, Don was on the floor. His lips were wet with saliva. He formed the words, "Apomorphine" with difficulty. As I knelt beside him, hoping I could help, a frigid mask of coma stiffened his face.

From far away I heard my cry, "Oh, God... God...God." I put my hands to my head. The heels of my hands pulled at my face, my fingernails dug into my scalp. I had to wake up. This was a nightmare.

I ran out the back door, down the frost-bound yard, into Leroy. With gentle firmness he set me aside and sprinted for the house.

I watched Leroy lift Don onto our bed. The door opened, and his nurse came in. "Nancy called me," she said.

"He'd be better off in a city hospital," Leroy said. "Better make it Duluth. That's his hospital. Fargo's closer, but he isn't going to be happy if he wakes up in Fargo. Get the ambulance." Then he turned to me, "Why don't you pack a bag for both of you? Hard to tell how long you'll be there."

Hal Swanson drove the ambulance. I was glad it was Hal. Don had once said he couldn't count the lakes he and Hal had fished as kids. Mary was there in starched white. She would go with us, riding up front. I sat with Don.

We'd been on the road an hour when Don started to sit up. It was the first time he'd moved. Raising his head, a fountain of green and yellow erupted from his mouth. I grabbed a towel to help him. "Oh, thank you, Lord! This is what he wanted to do." Relief spread through me.

I matched my breathing to his. I remembered the operation in Chicago, the breathing chart I'd made for him.

My breath caught and held, waiting for his next one. It didn't come. I couldn't believe it. I pushed my breath into his mouth. Nothing happened.

November 27, 1937. No helicopters cruised the highway. No paramedics. No life-support systems. Just death.

I laid my head on his heart. Stillness. Only stillness. My world was still and empty.

The brakes gripped, stopping the car. Mary was crying hysterically. I didn't raise my head from Don's breast. How few nights I had fallen asleep there.

Five hours had passed since we had awakened to a fair and sunny morning.

Mary clambered in beside me. She clutched my head to her pounding heart. "He's gone...he's gone!" she wailed. She had loved Don since the day of his birth. He was the son she never had. She spoke haltingly, "Dottie, we knew he couldn't make it. It was a massive cerebral hemorrhage." She turned to Hal, "We'd better go to Deer River. There's a doctor there. He'll have to sign the death certificate before we can go back." She turned to me again. "Don't you want to come up front?" she asked.

I shook my head. Hal closed the door. We drove on, no longer at breakneck speed with siren screaming. Time crawled around us. It didn't matter any more.

"You wait here in the ambulance," Mary said when we got to Deer River. "You'll have to answer some questions."

What questions? The doctor would have to certify that Don was dead before we could go home? I hadn't realized there were rules about dying.

Hal came back to sit with me. Mary went in to wait for the doctor. Resting his head against the side of the stretcher, Hal suddenly looked up. "Are you all right?" he asked.

What did he mean, was I all right? I didn't answer.

I had said the words without knowing it. They returned, "All things work together for good to them that love God, to them who are the called according to His purpose."

In Wheaton Chapel that night, God knew what I was committing myself to. I didn't. I had said, "You write the ticket, Lord. Do with me what you will." Had I been out of my mind?

How could Don's death possibly be one of those "things" that God would "work together for good"? How could I believe *that*, on *this* day?

Hal's shoulders moved in a silent sob.

"I'm all right," I said. My mind was stepping gingerly about, picking some thoughts as they came, rejecting others. I had assumed Don and I would have forty or fifty years together, but God knew all along we wouldn't. And yet...yet He had given us almost six wonderful years of belonging to each other, engaged four years, married two.

What had Job said? I mumbled the words, "The Lord gave, and the Lord hath taken away, blessed be the name of the Lord."[1]

"What is it?" Hal had a hungry look. "I've seen people sit where you are. Some of 'em have something like you do. They don't fall apart. It's not just religion; it's more than that. I know I don't have it. I'm scared." He fought for control. "I believe there's a God. Anybody with sense knows that, but how can you sit there and be calm when your life just went down the drain?" His voice was rising, "How can it be all right for God to deny people the years of skill and care that Don would have given them?"

"The Lord says if we hide His word in our hearts, it will keep us from sinning against Him.[2] I didn't know before how true that is, but just now when I couldn't think a thought for myself, I could feel God's Word being fed to me. The Holy Spirit does it; Jesus said He would."[3]

"Say the one you said before about 'the Lord gives.' "

"The Lord giveth, and the Lord taketh away, blessed be the name of the Lord." But listen to this one, "And we *know* that *all* things work together for good to them who love God, to them who are the called according to His purpose." I can't begin to know how that works right now. All I *do* know is that if I don't believe it, I'm calling God a liar. I can't do that."

In the clustering darkness, Mary and Dr. Banning opened the ambulance door. I answered his questions, and he said gently, "Mrs. Penheiter, you are welcome to use my phone to make any calls you need to."

It hadn't occurred to me that I must call Moth. Oh, Dear God, *how* could I tell her?

I trudged up the long steep stairs to the doctor's office. *If all the hard things in life were phys-*

*ical, like this climb, it would be much easier,* I thought.

Hal's face came before me. Who knows the price of one eternal soul? Not I. I know that heaven gave all it had. And I knew that Don would have given his life for Hal if Hal had been drowning. God knew. I knew. somehow that in the ambulance where Don's human life had ended, Hal's eternal life had begun.

I called home first. Daddy's warm voice said, "Dot, are you all right?" He could tell.

"Daddy. It's Don. He's. . .gone."

"Don? Did you say Don is *gone*? Oh, no!"

"Yes. He died just a little while ago," I whispered.

"Mother and I will come. We'll come to Bemidji. I'll wire you when to meet us. Now listen, my dear, this is no mistake. I don't know how Don died, but I know that he couldn't have died unless the Lord either directed it or permitted it. Everything is on schedule with God. Don't forget that."

"But he's *gone*, Daddy!"

"I know. How well I know, but you listen to me. I want you to read Romans 8:28 over and over again until it is burned into your soul. God never says anything He does not mean. The Lord bless you, Honey, He does, and He will. We love you. We're coming."

I knew he had hung up, but I stayed there listening. I felt nearer to him than I ever had in my whole life, and I needed him more. He *knew*.

Mama had died when we were little kids. He knew what it was like.

I stood there by the phone, fending off the job of telling Moth. What could I say? Euphemisms don't cushion death. Suddenly I remembered that she was not home. She was in Glasgow, Montana, visiting her other brother, also a doctor. Thank God. She was not alone.

Wearily I picked up the phone. My whole being strained to insulate her from the shock.

Warm surprise hung in her voice when she answered. "What a *nice* Thanksgiving surprise! How are you? And how is our favorite doctor?"

"Moth, he's gone. He's gone to be with the Lord."

"Oh, my dear! I knew this would happen some day, but not so soon. Well, there's rejoicing in heaven, you can be sure of that. But you. How are *you*?" The warmth never wavered. She wasn't thinking about her loss, only mine.

Mary took the phone from me. I didn't hear any more. All I could think was, *Why, God, why? Why did this have to happen? You say You can work it together for good. Maybe for the world, and for You, but not for me.*

Mary put down the phone. She was crying again. "They will start tonight. Clarence and Louise will drive her, but she says the snow is so bad it'll be a long trip."

Darkness fell shortly after we left Deer River. It began to snow lightly. How many times had Don and I walked together with snowflakes on our eyelashes and love in our hearts? I could close my eyes and feel his cold cheek against mine and his arms hard around me.

Outward calm like a huge earthen dam kept me from unveiling the grief that bruised my soul. Dr. Banning had said, "Don't be afraid to cry. It would be good for you to cry..."

Leroy was at the car when we drove up to the hospital. He covered his own loss beneath a veneer of bedside manner, hard-trained by repeated lessons in heartbreak. He gave short, clipped orders: "Dorothy, you go right upstairs and take a hot bath. Mary, take care of her. I'll be up to give her a sedative shortly."

He *knew* what a hot bath would do to me. As I turned on the water, the tears gathered and fell, slowly at first. I settled into the hot tub. I wanted to slide under and stay. I didn't want to go on. Waves of self-pity rolled over me. I wallowed in them.

Any idea that God was in charge fled from me. I did not want to remember what Daddy had said about reading Romans 8:28. Things were *not* on schedule with God. How could He have scheduled *this*? A hard fist grew in me and became red-hot rebellion. I recoiled from the thought that a just and righteous and loving God could do this to me—to Leroy—to Mary—to Bagley. I mutinied.

The convulsion and revulsion that shook me were a fury of outrage—against God. This was clearly not an act of God. He let Don have the fatal flu. He saved him long enough for us to fall in love.

Why couldn't He have taken him when Eunice died, or his father? Why mess my life up?

But, according to C.S. Lewis, "A man can no more diminish God's glory by refusing to worship Him than a lunatic can put out the sun by scribbling the word 'darkness' on the walls of his cell."[4]

When the water began to cool, I returned to reality. I stepped out, wrapped myself in a towel and sat there watching the tub empty. The water disappeared. *My life went down the drain today, too,* I thought.

Leroy came into the room after I'd crawled into bed. "Give me an arm," he said with hypo poised. His eyes were full of hurt. How could I deduce what this day had cost him? He said, "Mary's gone to bed. I doubt if she has the grit that you have to take this. She'll need your help, and I will too. We don't know your Lord." He turned abruptly and left.

The next morning when I awoke, I lay quietly for a few minutes. I was disoriented. Why was I here in Leroy and Mary's guest room? Then I remembered.

I dressed slowly and went out into the bright kitchen where I had first met Mary. We had come in June and sunshine. Today was November 28, cold and forbidding. Thanksgiving weekend. Bitterness filled my soul. I wanted to go back to my room and stay there. Never come out. I wondered what it would be like to have no memory. But that would take away all the good memories, too. I didn't want that.

The comic section of the Sunday paper lay on the breakfast table. Garish colors grinned hideously. I stared at them. How could people read papers like that, and laugh on a day like this? The radio filled the air with the labored humor of a disc jockey. I turned it off and went back to my room.

Late that evening the door opened in the darkened hallway. Moth came up the last steps toward me. Her eyes were black. Anguish carved her features. But she exuded a serenity I didn't possess. Her inner peace was not shattered. It was manifest. She had been prepared for this. I was caught off-balance.

On Monday morning, Leroy and I met Mother and Daddy in Bemidji. The sounds of the 6:30 train were muffled by snow and wind. Daddy came first. He turned to help Mother down, then he held me tightly in his strong arms. He smelled of bay rum, and his glasses were steaming up as his breath rose in the freezing air. Mother was fragrant and bountifully cheerful. She always was. Stars were still visible in the half light of the coming day. Not a word had been spoken about Don.

Driving back to Bagley, Leroy gave the folks a complete medical report. I could hear Don again explaining that the flu weakened the vascular system. All three had died the same. Don's father's thrombosis was coronary, Eunice's pulmonary, Don's cerebral. I hadn't known he was living on borrowed time, but wait—I *had* known. Don had told me on that ride to Minneapolis.

The funeral was held in the church across the street from our house, the first funeral. The second was in Fargo, his former home.

I was drifting when I heard the minister say, "Have you ever walked up close to the backdrop of a woods scene, such as might be used in a high school play?"

He had my attention. I'd helped paint backdrops for literary society programs at Wheaton. His voice came through again. "Close to it, you noticed how ugly the streaks and splotches of black or brown were, didn't you? But from the back of the auditorium, you saw the whole thing from a different perspective. Without the dark spots, there would be no picture. We are too close. God sees it from the back of the auditorium, a finished piece. All things taken together, it is good, necessary."

Those words again.

On the ride back to Bagley, Daddy said things in a way that made me know he'd been waiting for the right time. "Dot, right after your mother died, I felt awfully sorry for myself, but I finally found some answers."

"How?"

Digging facts out of the Word. It says in 2 Peter 3:8, "...one day is with the Lord as a thousand years, and a thousand years as one day." I figured He meant that one day in heaven is equal to a thousand days on earth. I got out my slide rule and figured that if I lived to be seventy, your mother would have been in heaven forty-one minutes."

"Help me figure mine." It came to forty-five minutes. Three quarters of an hour. "Why, Don won't have time to take in the glory of the Lord, and I'll be right there beside him!"

He won't have time to be lonely for me. That had been one of my problems. Surely he was missing me as much as I was him. But now I knew he wouldn't have time.

A strange new energy stirred me. I was alive. I was warm and breathing. That meant God had something for me to do. That's why he'd left me here. I wouldn't be lonely.

Daddy read my thoughts. He broke in, "Don't ever underestimate the power of loneliness. Just because you licked it at one moment, don't count it as your last battle."

If I'd only known how prophetic that was.

When we reached Bagley, a letter from Don's insurance company was on the hall table. His insurance was no longer rated. The company was happy to inform him that he was a standard risk. Actuarially, he would live to a ripe old sixty-five or seventy.

# PART II

## THE GROWING: Romans 8:28 Examined

*"Trust in the Lord with all thine heart;
and lean not unto thine own understanding. In all thy ways acknowledge him, and
he shall direct thy paths." Proverbs 3:6.*

# From Grace To Grace

Though I walk through the valley
And shadows are nigh,
I'm assured He'll be waiting
On the other side.
My heart can't be troubled
Neither be afraid.
I'm clinging to the comfort
Of a promise He made.
And from grace to grace I go, from day to day
His mercy carries me on from grace to grace.
He is leading me, leading me, leading me home.
Though I walk through the valley
And shadows are deep,
At the end there's a mansion
Waiting there for me.
I shall not be frightened
Neither be alarmed.
Here beside the still waters
He keeps me from harm.
And from grace to grace I go, from day to day
His mercy carries me on from grace to grace.
He is leading me, leading me, leading me home.

● *1979 Neva Thompson*

---

## Struggle

"Say, Miss, what d' y' want me t' do with all these yams and yellies down in the fruit cellar?" The strong Scandinavian voice came from the open trap door in the pantry.

"I guess you'd better bring them up here, Hilda. Doc and Mrs. Larson will be able to use them," I answered from the living room where we were packing the china.

Daddy, Mother and I had been working, dismantling the house for three days. The neighbors helped and Mary came when she could. We were taking our nest apart bit by bit. And bit by bit, we were taking my life apart, too. Nothing was easy about this job.

Everything would go into storage. Mother, Daddy and I were leaving for Minneapolis in the morning.

The season of Thanksgiving had turned toward Christmas. I would be home for the holidays. After that, I had promised to spend the month of January in Fargo with Moth. I wasn't sure what would follow, but perhaps I'd settle down in the warmth of the Wheaton College family and take some courses at the college. Something. Keep busy.

As we stood waiting for the train to come in, Mary said, "You've lost only Don. Leroy and I are losing both of you." I hadn't thought of their suffering as much as I should have.

The train speeding south passed through frozen fields. Only six months before, Don and I had ridden north over that same roadbed in the fullness of reunion after all the times of separation. I had been brimful of questions as Don had taken me into Bagley for the first time. The questions had all been answered. Bagley was a closed chapter. So was the warmth and love and sense of completeness Don had brought me.

I looked out of the window at the tranquil land. It was cold but peaceful. The geese, the ducks, the mallards had all gone south. Instinct saved them from suffering. What were those lines of William Cullen Bryant's about the waterfowl? I could remember only snatches:

> He, who from zone to zone,
> Guides through the boundless sky thy certain flight,
> In the long way that I must trace alone,
> Will lead my steps aright.

"Read Romans 8:28," Daddy had said the afternoon Don died. "Read it and study it." I opened my Bible, which I seemed to need near me as I never had before. I read the words again. If I could only be sure that the end *would* be good, then I could bear to look ahead. I was resisting God again. I was not trusting Him.

The idea of being alone, unmarried, unloved was a terrible prospect. Look forward to it? Not me.

In all those years of waiting, I had lived for the future. I had simply patted my foot and written letters while time went by. How long had that future lasted? One month of camping with plaster in our hair, two meals using the best china, one meal on the dining room table.

I needed to draw lessons from this experience. "Live one day at a time; don't always live in the future" was one lesson I had to remember. "Just because God gives you something doesn't necessarily mean that He'll allow you to have it indefinitely" was another.

I loved God, but I had loved Don more. I had leaned on him, not on God. God had taken me up on my declaration that night after the Wheaton prayer meeting. I had meant it, but had I really counted the cost?

The growth period of my life was beginning.

I either believed what God said or I didn't. I could not straddle the fence. He said He could make all things — all the bad things, too — work together — mesh, interact, interweave — for good on earth and in eternity. He *did* say that; how could I contradict Him?

I was back to that first flash of insight when Hal and I had sat in the ambulance waiting for Dr. Banning. If I didn't believe the fact of the promise, I *was* calling God a liar. There didn't seem to be a way around that. *Wanting* to believe was not sufficient. I either did or I didn't.

I was slow to realize with C. S. Lewis that pain "plants the flag of truth within the fortress of a rebel soul."[1]

One day I would agree with Thomas Aquinas,

who said of suffering that it was a thing not good in itself, but a thing which might have certain goodness in particular circumstances.[2] It took growth to come to that conclusion.

On the train I read and read the Bible. All other reading material was trivia. My heart, my soul, my spirit were like raw hamburger. A meat-grinder experience, that's what it was. I felt so torn apart, so fragile. I wanted to die and join Don. I drew closer and closer to the Lord. My treasure was in heaven, and my heart yearned to follow.

Every time I'd meet an old friend who loved Don, the tears surfaced. Grief was new and sorrow joined sorrow.

In Wheaton at Duntons', the memories flooded back. The atmosphere of the college permeated the house from the front door, where we entered, to the back door that Don had always used. The entire upper story was a men's dormitory. In the basement the ping-pong table was set up permanently. This was my home-away-from-home, too.

The evening we arrived Marg told us about the memorial service that had been held for Don at the college. "The theme of the service was beautiful," she said.

"What was it?" I knew she was going to recount some tribute that would bring tears.

"Precious in the sight of the Lord is the death of His saints," she said.

I recoiled. Precious? His death was precious to God? I couldn't believe that was so. But it was in the Bible, Psalm 116:15. Though I probably had

read it before, I had never *seen* it. It was an idea
too hard to evaluate in the light of my loss and my
dread of life without Don. God was glad that he
was dead!

All evening I was troubled. The verse moved
in my mind as though it were a living thing. It was
alive! Hebrews 4:12 says "For the word of God is
quick (alive) and powerful, and sharper than any
two-edged sword, piercing even to the dividing
asunder of soul and spirit, and of the joints and
marrow, and is a discerner of the thoughts and in-
tents of the heart." I knew these verses. I'd gone
through them, but for the first time they were sig-
nificant. They had new force and meaning.

Marg's excitement as she told about the
memorial service was catching. She said, "It was
a celebration of life, not a mourning of loss! This
will thrill you: at least twenty young people met the
Lord as a direct result of Don's death, and fifteen
determined to go into medicine to pick up the torch
he dropped. How many Christian lives have that
kind of harvest?" she asked.

New perspectives, new understanding was filling in the cracks every day. I searched the Scripture as I never had in all my life before. It was the
link to heaven. But then, as I lay in bed that night
and thought, it was hard to believe that all of Don's
dearness, his love of Jesus Christ, all that he was
in life was of less value in God's sight than was his
death. I drifted off to sleep recognizing that I had
my nose in the black spot of the backdrop.

## New Hope, New Happiness

"My, it must be nice to get things just for your-self for a change," my cousin blurted out as we sat around the Christmas tree. I felt as though a bucket of ice cold water had been dumped on me. I was so fractured that whole people didn't feel comfortable. But making conversation isn't the answer.

After the month of December at home, I left for Fargo and Moth. The weather in Fargo, 20 or 30 below zero, was not conducive to walking. I was alone in Moth's apartment most of the time as she was teaching at the business college.

The month with her had a fantasy air about it. Time stood still. I ate kadota figs and homemade bread without thinking of the future. I was soak-ing up the faith and patience that God had work-ed within Moth in the years of hardship and denial she had experienced. They hadn't dried her out, but rather supplied her with a sweet serenity I ad-mired and yearned for. I knew the source, and I sought Him.

I came to realize that while a great harvest had been reaped in Don's going, the other half of God's plan for us would be worked out in my remaining years. I must live as though I believed the promise of Romans 8:28. I couldn't do that if I didn't truly believe it and take God at His word. I was back to square one. A promise is only as good as the one who makes it. The more I read the Word, the more sure I was that the Lord had never failed to keep one of His promises.

I found I was beginning to believe my beliefs and doubt my doubts. That was a switch. It had been the other way around, a trap: believing my doubts and doubting my beliefs.

By mid-February I was back in Wheaton, settled in my old room with Pop Hosler and his daughter Mary. They were a necessary part of my healing.

One day I received a call from the manager of the college dining halls. Two years working with foods in Chicago had given me entre to the job of manager of the New Dorm Dining Hall. No happenstance, this. I was gainfully employed, and engrossed in business; I could forget for hours at a time.

People began to accept me for myself, not as a broken piece of a pair. It was like our previous separation. The separation *had* been a blessing after all.

One evening when the other girls in the house were out on dates, I slid into my desk chair and pulled a clean sheet of stationery toward me. "Dear Heart," I wrote, "I miss you so horribly. Can you possibly know how lonely the days are for me? And the nights. I love you, Darling. I'll never love anyone else..."

The tears dripped freely as I wrote. It felt good to cry, to weep my heart out. "Oh, God! Why did you have to take him? Why couldn't we have had a baby? Why do I have to go on living? What for? Oh, God. Oh, God. Oh, God."

I threw myself on the bed and sobbed, indulging myself, my self-pity. Once I thought I heard the door close downstairs. The girls would be coming home. Pitching the sound down a few decibels, I got up, shed my clothes and left them in a heap, threw on a nightgown and crawled back into bed, and cried the night through.

The next morning bloodshot eyes returned my mirror stare. I ran my hand over puffy lips and splashed cold water on a splotched face. I was disgusted with myself. Back in my room, I knelt by my bed. "Lord, with Your help, I'll never do that again. It does no one any good. I give up. I've tried, but I can't make things work together for anything. I want to love You no matter what. Will You take over? Please."

Many years later I learned that God does not help those who help themselves. He helps the helpless. As long as I would go one step further in my own strength, God would let me try. When I finally realized that I'm not smart enough to solve my own problems, I could give up, relax, let go, and let God take over.

Three summers later I was food supervisor at George Williams College Camp in Wisconsin. It was my summer for disasters of one kind or another. Watching the camp nurse bind up my assistant's fingers, nearly cut off in the cabbage shredder, I passed out and fell back on the concrete floor. Concussion. Rest. The food service went on minus Number One and Number Two. A week later as I was taking inventory in the walk-in freezer, a stainless steel steam-table pan full of frozen fish dislodged and slid off the top shelf. It missed my head but plunged a cold, hard corner into the center of my right foot.

The idea that "all things work together for good" was a reflex with me now. I still couldn't believe that *good* would eventuate from such unnecessary pain. So many things that happened to me seemed "unnecessary." I'd find myself muttering, "Lord, this didn't *have* to happen, did it? I didn't *need* the concussion or the torn foot."

So I thought. How little I knew about God's plan for my life. I forgot my commitment to Him more often than I remembered it.

I continued to look at life from the human viewpoint. I didn't have enough of God's Word in my soul to see events from his frame of reference. Gradually I came to see that every day was a part of that working-together, and that it wasn't just the happenings of the day, but what they effected in me that counted. When I hurt, my aloneness was more biting, and I drew nearer my best friend, Jesus Christ.

Back in Wheaton for the school year, I received a call from Murray Brewer, the YMCA purchasing agent for the Chicago area. It was Christmastime, and the Brewers came out to go to the Sunday afternoon performance of the *Messiah* with me.

During the intermission Murray leaned across his wife and said, "Dorothy, how would you like to be the restaurant manager of the YMCA Hotel in Chicago?"

Bombshell!

Four dining rooms, 150 employees, 6000 meals a day, he said. I said I couldn't do it; he said I could. I went to Chicago, was interviewed, and soon was on my way, bag and baggage.

Work is healing, but not if it crowds out the Lord. Twelve or thirteen hours of work a day stretched to fifteen and more at times. Just getting acquainted with the staff took time. By the end of the year, the restaurant was in the black with a $30,000 profit instead of the $8,000 it had lost each of the three previous years. The main reason was that I was honest. It made a difference.

One night I finished late in my office and was passing through the lobby on my way to the elevator that would boost me to the 18th floor where I lived. One of the hotel cashiers, Lloyd Galde, said as we passed, "Would you like to bowl for an hour and get that restaurant look off your face?" *Smart mouth!* I thought, but I went.

On our way home, we stopped for hamburgers. As we waited for them, Lloyd said, "Do you ever expect to marry again?"

"No," I answered. "That's a closed chapter. I settled that before I came to Chicago, and I'm too busy to reopen the matter."

"Aw, c'mon, I was just kidding. I know you're performing a miracle in the restaurant end of the hotel. McClow dances a polka every morning when he sees the figures. They've never been so good.

You're a lot younger and prettier than the former manager anyway," he finished lamely.

"Flattery will get you everywhere," I said as I bit into a juicy hamburger after decorating it with mustard.

"We have much in common," Lloyd went on. "I was engaged to a girl back in LaCrosse, where I took my first year of college. I worked my fingernails to the armpits saving up money to buy the engagement ring. Took it to her at Christmas and found she was out with another guy to whom she was also engaged. Marriage is for the birds."

The next morning I found a little note in my mailbox. The following day another, and the next. It was habit-forming. Lloyd was bringing laughter into my life.

Things were going too well. I should have expected a problem of some kind, but I didn't. In the beauty shop one evening, the hair dryer descended on my head as I was rising from the chair. The metal piece encasing the light cut deep into my scalp. Blood all over the place.

The hotel doctor sewed it up, and my secretary took me home. By this time I had moved out of the hotel and was living in a lakeshore apartment on the south side.

The first Sunday after the accident, Moth came from Evanston, and Marg Dunton came from Wheaton to take care of the invalid. Late in the afternoon, Lloyd appeared, carrying a florist's box about three feet long. Moth was gentle but direct as she gave him the third degree.

His home: Superior, Wisconsin. His short range goal: finish school at George Williams. His long range goal: become a YMCA secretary.

He left for Washington, D.C. on a previously planned vacation before I had repaired sufficiently to be back at my desk. A card came from him a few days later. It said: "Either the Washington Monument isn't all it's cracked up to be, or nothing looks good unless you're looking at it with me."

When he returned, we spent the first Sunday afternoon in the park by Lake Michigan. The birds were singing, the bushes were in bloom, the air was soft and warm. We sat on a stone bench facing the lake.

"It's been a long week," he began, resting his arm across the back of the bench, behind me. "Why did I go?"

"To see Washington, I thought."

"That isn't all I saw," he said as he turned to face me. "I saw myself alone, without you for years ahead, and I didn't like it." He paused and looked at me with a new look. "Dorothy, will you marry me?"

Before I answered, he rushed on, "You are different from any girl I have ever known, and I know what that difference is. It's your relationship to Christ. I knew that before you would consider me seriously, I'd have to get right with Him. I did that while I was gone. It was a struggle—giving up the old me, and there's still plenty of me left, but I feel right with the universe for the first time in my life. Whether you love me enough to marry me or not,

I shall always be thankful that I saw Christ in you and fell in love with Him."

Almost four years had elapsed since Don's death. Would the hunger for love and companionship be satisfied in Lloyd? Being with him had become addicting. He was such dear company. He was three and a half years younger than I. An inward struggle claimed much of my time as I thought about us. Lloyd wasn't six feet tall like Don. He wasn't blond. He was but a few inches taller than I. It may seem stupid, but that bothered me. No more high heels for me. I tried to think of a marriage from his viewpoint. Would he always feel insecure because I had finished college and he had not, yet? Were we daft to shut our eyes to the differences?

Love is supposed to be blind, but blind to what? To such disparity? I was older than he; women mature earlier; I had been married; therefore I must be more mature than the years that separated us. And so it went, round and round. I couldn't envision the days ahead without Lloyd, and yet I could see knotty problems in the offing if we joined forces.

While I was having second and third thoughts, after committing myself, Lloyd took the job of assistant manager of the Kenosha Hotel, in Kenosha, Wisconsin. Proximity departed. He was absent from the scene at the YMCA Hotel.

I missed him more than I thought I could. I felt as though an arm had been amputated. I wasn't whole without him. Discovery! I spent more time thinking about him now that I couldn't se him every day.

We had decided to look for an apartment in Evanston, halfway between our places of work. One night around Thanksgiving after unsuccessful apartment hunting, we stopped in at a tea shop for some hot chocolate. He pulled a letter from his pocket and placed it in front of me. It was his draft notice.

The world blew up in my face. It had been just a dream. Maybe I wasn't supposed to marry again. Maybe the Lord was telling me to stay single. Irrational thoughts, to be sure. What was the message here? One more hurdle. Life is made up of hurdles. You don't sink to the ground in front of them; you strengthen and go over.

Out of the mist that clouded my eyes, I remembered my love for Don. He was gone. Would Lloyd go, too? He was being drafted into a peacetime army, but that could change in 24 hours. I had thought God was filling up my life again. Maybe I misread the signs.

I was on the elevated train headed toward the South Shore before I summoned up Romans 8:28. As I looked out of the window, I saw the lights of Chicago. Huge flakes of snow were silently covering the city. Through tears I watched the snow begin to edge the trees and buildings and dampen the streets. I wondered at the fact that so often the white, the cold, the loneliness came together.

As day followed day, I began to unravel my problem. I was not taking life a day at a time. I needed to do that. It was no good living in the future as I had before Don and I were married. God promises strength for the day—"As thy days, so shall thy strength be"[1]. He didn't promise to give me strength today for next week.

"God has something for me to do today," I would tell myself every morning. Each minute, each hour I must live up to the light I had. Each day I must take in the Word of God to be prepared for the day's dilemmas. There are no part-time Christians. Whatever the assignment, if I did it as unto Him and not as unto men, I would be pleasing the almighty God. I would be serving Him.

Not wanting to be a draftee, Lloyd enlisted in the Air Force. The USAF did not accept married men. Our Christmas wedding was off. The twin blue covert cloth suits we had ordered for the wedding would be nice to have, but they wouldn't be our wedding suits. This we knew when we said "Good night" on a Saturday night in December. Saturday, December 6, 1941.

After church Sunday noon, we had dinner at the Palmer House. I ate in my restaurant every day; it was fun to dine out. I had work to do in the afternoon, and Lloyd would soon be on his way back to Kenosha.

Lloyd had ordered for us, and we sat there holding hands under the table cloth when the radio music stopped. The announcer said, "News has just been received that Pearl Harbor was bombed by Japanese planes this morning. Most of the fleet was in the harbor. Many of our planes were on the ground. It is impossible to know at this time how many hundreds, possibly thousands of American lives have been lost. It is expected that Congress will declare war against the Japanese Empire within hours."

WAR! Lloyd's stretch in the Air Force would not be just practice. He would be going where I could not follow. I would be afraid for him, hating the distance and the unknowns that would separate us. Numbly I realized the separation was the pattern of my life. I'd be writing letters again instead of settling down in that cottage with the white picket fence.

We went home as planned at Christmas. The holiday was subdued. We didn't know whether Mason or Joe or Paul would have to go. The next day the whole family met in Buffalo for dinner at Lorenzo's and a picture show called *Dumbo*. As we sat around a long table waiting to be served, Joe spoke up, "Say, I see by the papers that the Air Force is accepting married men now."

*"What?"* Lloyd surged out of his chair.

"Wait a minute," Joe raised an arm to fend him off. "What did I say to bring this on?"

Lloyd didn't answer. He was halfway to the door, going for a *Buffalo Evening News*.

We'd kept our heartbreak to ourselves, so no one but Daddy and Mother knew why we weren't getting married.

Lillian said, "What's the matter with him?"

"He just wants to marry me, that's all," I said.

"Here it is!" he said beaming as he came back.

I hadn't seen that look since before the draft notice. He dashed to the phone booth near the table and called Chicago. The recruiting office would still be open there.

By this time our dinners were being served. The waitress stood by Lloyd's place, holding his dinner and looking helpless.

Mason spoke up, "You just put that down. We'll eat it. He won't know the difference."

The barbecued chicken was still hot when Lloyd came back from the telephone booth. He had a banana smile on his face. "Well, shall we call this a pre-wedding supper?"

"What did he say?" Now I didn't care about eating.

"Said 'Go to it' in words that only a first sergeant can pronounce," Lloyd reported, squeezing my arm.

We were married on New Year's Day. Lloyd and I, dressed in our matching suits, stood in front of the fireplace in the living room. My shoulder was heavy with gardenias.

We returned to Chicago by train on the 5th of January. Lloyd helped me move back to the hotel. On January 27, he left for Kelly Field in San Antonio, Texas.

A week or so later Moth came down from Evanston to have dinner with me. After eating we went upstairs to my room. She laid her Bible open on the table and pointed to Matthew 18:19. I read: "Again I say unto you that if two of you shall agree on earth as touching any thing that they shall ask, it shall be done for them of My Father which is in Heaven."

She said, "I want to covenant with you in asking God to spare Lloyd's life, whether he goes overseas or not; wherever he is, that he may return to you."

Stunned at her generosity, I still had difficulty. "But Moth, I thought a prayer should always say, 'Not my will but Thine.' I don't know whether we have the right to ask for his life."

"You either believe the Scripture or you don't," she said.

Even though I had known the Lord for probably twenty-five chronological years, I still had a long way to go. I know now that a prayer doesn't always truthfully reflect the desire behind it. God hears the petition; He knows what prompted it. Sometimes He answers the petition as He did when Israel asked for a king. but he left the desire unanswered.[2] Israel wanted to be like other nations. God's chosen people would never be like others.

Sometimes God doesn't answer the petition; He gives the desire rather than the stated prayer. Dr. R.B. Thieme, Jr., a pastor in Houston, Texas points out that in the case of Abram's request that God spare Sodom and Gomorrah, he *did* answer the desire: Lot's safety.

Moth's desire was for my happiness. God answered both the petition and the desire. He preserved Lloyd's life although the odds were great.

Have you noticed that when you invest in someone or something by praying, you are often part of the answer? You begin to pray for the work of a particular missionary, and before you know it, you feel you must support him with your money as well.

I agreed to covenant with Moth about Lloyd's life. I had no idea what it would cost me.

In May my professional career came to an unprofessional halt. I was pregnant. Lloyd had left on January 27. The months of February, March, and April provided a new experience: morning sickness. I looked at the world through a bilious green haze from daybreak to darkness. I would be fine as I rode down the elevator from my private eyrie, but the second I opened the door to the cafeteria on my way back to my office, the breakfast odors assailed my nostrils. I had to race to reach the proper place in time. I was captive to the changes that were occurring in me. After a week in bed to prevent miscarriage late in April, I took a train for Buffalo. My career as a restaurateur was finished.

October 20th was the target date. Mother and Daddy were gearing up for a 25th wedding anniversary on that very day. Lloyd was coming from Pine Bluff, Arkansas, on a 15-day pass. I planned the anniversary reception, but our firstborn had other plans.

Sunday, October 18 was busy. Evangelistic meetings at church went on all day. I felt great, in more ways than one. At midnight the amniotic fluid broke. I was ignorant of the fact that this could preclude a 'dry birth,' which would be painful. It did and it was. Twenty-one hours later Peter Mason took center stage in person. He was exhausted, but he had a bulldog hold on life. He still has.

When Peter was six months old, he and I flew to San Bernardino, California. Lloyd was stationed at Victorville, in training to be a glider pilot. Frequently he would come home to us on a three-day pass and play civilian. It was good to be together again.

In May we followed Lloyd to Lubbock, Texas. By Christmas Pete and I went back to Hamburg to celebrate the holidays and to welcome another little Galde. I had to have the bone in my nose windowed to relieve sinus congestion the day before Danny was born on the 5th of January.

As Lloyd's departure for Europe drew close, the tightness around my heart increased. We'd be back to letter writing again. I appreciated anew the biblical truth that in heaven there will be no parting. Heaven made me think of Don. I wondered if he knew that as much as I had loved him and tried to be all that a wife should be, I was trying harder the second time. I was acutely aware that Lloyd might be killed in action. I remembered the covenant with Moth; I knew how much Peter and Danny would need their father, but only God could know what was the best for us in the long run— the eternal run.

Lloyd came home, and we went house-hunting again. Nothing was available in Hamburg, so we drove up to Forestville where Lillian and Paul lived. Forestville was about forty miles from Buffalo, a little country town surrounded by vineyards. We rented Old Doc Hutchinson's house, just a creek and a house away from Paul and Lillian. Loda, the doctor's widow, lived in the front three rooms that had been the doctor's office. We had the rest of the house, upstairs and downstairs. Paul pastored the Baptist Church, the same church Grandpa Spencer had shepherded fifty years earlier.

The furniture Don and I had picked out in Minneapolis in another lifetime fitted right into the Forestville house. I painted walls and woodwork in between baby care, washing, unpacking, grocery shopping and gardening. Lloyd came back on his way to embarkation in New York City. He had a week.

My sinuses were a mess. I guess I'd pushed the paint brush too hard and too long. The doctor prescribed rest. I always have to chuckle at such prescriptions for mothers. However, Lloyd rose to the challenge. He said, "Honey, don't worry. I'm a good cook. [And he is.] I can take care of the boys. Relax; it may be your last chance." He patted my pillow and made me comfortable on the living room sofa.

By the third day, he had slowed to a crawl. As I was luxuriously reclining on my bed of ease that morning, I looked up when I heard a noise. Lloyd was coming in from the kitchen, through the dining room on his hands and knees, weaving with weariness. He gripped a white flag between his teeth.

"Honey, I surrender," he groaned. "I'll go fight the war and leave the tough job for you."

Pounding head or not, I dissolved in laughter.

# CHAPTER
## SIX

## Disaster

Lloyd's troopship had been gone for several weeks before word came of his safe arrival in Europe. All through the summer, mail came several times a week, but as fall approached, communications broke down. I was writing daily, and he had always done so. I couldn't figure out what had happened. The long silence began to get on my nerves. I couldn't sleep nights. I was back to my close walk with Christ. Sometimes.

Before dark, I would bathe the babies and put them to bed. Then I'd go out and sit on the steps and breathe the sweetness of the clover and honeysuckle. I would walk along the creek trying to tire myself sufficiently to sleep. Loda listened for the children.

Daytimes weren't so difficult. But at night, I didn't want to go to our room, to bed—alone—until I was exhausted.

Would Lloyd come back? It isn't true that lightning doesn't strike twice in the same place. I'd seen silos by big red barns hit three times in the same place. I was living in the future again.

Moth and I had made a pact, but I didn't really believe that God would spare Lloyd's life simply because two of us had asked for it. How could He run the world that way?

I had my eyes on the situation, not on the Lord. I was feeling sorry for myself right up to the eyebrows. No way could I say "Thank you" to God. In order to do that, I'd have to embrace Romans 8:28 to the core of my soul.

After church on Sundays, the children and I would go to Paul and Lillian's for dinner. Their support was indispensable. I didn't know how Lloyd was or where he was.

Lillian usually stopped on weekdays when she went to town. One morning she brought the paper with her. The headlines shrieked **BUFFALO 800 POLIO CASES**. It was the summer of 1944. I was bathing Danny when she came. He was so round and pink and darling. The thought of children like him suffering the agony of infantile paralysis made me cower.

I shivered as I responded to her news, "I'm not going to take the boys out shopping any more at all. I've been putting netting over their carriage, but I'll feel safer if they're here at home. I think flies could carry it, don't you?"

"They don't seem to know. Flies certainly could. Is there anything I can get you?" she asked.

"Don't believe so. Remember, you're all coming for dinner Thursday night," I said.

"Right. See you," she closed the screen door as she went out.

They came Thursday night. We had a good time even though my head had ached all afternoon. As we finished the dishes, Lillian said, "Is anything wrong, Dot? You're not your usual cheerful self."

"I've had a miserable headache all afternoon.

It feels as though the top would blow off if I move much."

"Let me get Pete ready for bed before I go," she said as she went to call him. Her nearness and thoughtfulness took the edge from my loneliness. Paul, Jack, Annette, and Eddie were in the living room playing a game with Pete.

Soon the little boys were ready for bed and the Robinsons filed out the dining room door onto the side porch. Jack pulled me down for a big kiss. "That was a wonderful supper, Aunt Dot," he said.

"You're sweet," I hugged him. I leaned against the door and watched them as they straggled off the porch.

The bedrooms were upstairs. Pete and I made the trip up. He said his prayers, especially remembering his daddy. I went back down for Danny; I took more aspirin while I was down there.

After he was in bed, I crawled into our big bed by myself. It was scarcely nine o'clock.

After I'd been asleep a short while, I woke because my legs ached so, particularly the right leg from knee to hip. I rubbed it. The pain didn't lessen. Finally I inched my throbbing legs out of bed and located the heating pad. I turned it on high, hoping it would cover the pain.

At six the next morning, I took Danny downstairs for his early bottle. It was a frightening trip. As I stepped down each step, I sensed powerlessness. My legs might not support me one more step. I couldn't put Danny down, but I envisioned a plunge down the steep stairway for both of us.

Ultimately I reached the living room. I deposited him as quickly as I could, and fell on to the divan beside him.

The pain in my legs became more intense as I tended him. It was as though a piping hot griddle was being held firmly on the front of my legs above the knees.

Remembering the morning in Bagley when Don had been up all night, I waited until eight to call the doctor.

He came in an hour. He drove from Silver Creek. No doctors were left in Forestville. They'd all gone to war.

He was puzzled. Two weeks earier, I had called him because numbness had rendered my right arm, my face and tongue insensible. I thought then it was polio. He said, "Nerves!"

This time it was raw, searing pain.

After he examined me, he said, "Don't move off this couch today or tonight, Dorothy."

He called Lillian for help. She was tied up with out-of-town guests. He kept on calling until he found my friend Marilyn. She was there in less than ten minutes. He didn't leave until she was in charge.

"Just forget the children," she said as she started for the kitchen to get Pete's breakfast. "I'll take care of them. Try to sleep."

The medicine the doctor left put me to sleep. When night came, Marilyn brought the electric blanket. It helped. The next morning Marilyn was feeding the boys when the doctor pulled into the drive.

"How are you feeling this morning?" he said hopefully.

"Not so hot," was the best I could do.

"Raise your right leg," he directed.

I tried. It wouldn't move. A cold dread settled in the pit of my stomach.

"Raise your left leg," he ordered.

Slowly it came up about six inches. Then it sank down.

"Can you sit up?"

"Yes." I could. I pulled myself up to a sitting position.

"Put your head between your knees," he commanded.

I bent forward full of confidence. My head would not go down. My back was stiff. My neck was rigid.

He went to the phone, I supposed to call his office. He wouldn't talk, except pleasantries. A communication vacuum surrounded me. Both of us preferred not to face what might be true.

In forty-five minutes, another doctor arrived from Silver Creek. They asked me to sit up and bend forward as far as I could. They scrubbed the area they intended to prick to desensitize the place where they would take a spinal tap. The second doctor had a microscope. They put the slide under the lens. Deafening silence.

I could hear Floyd Pattyson next door mowing the lawn. Pete was out there, calling to Floyd and running alongside the mower. In the kitchen Danny was gurgling and playing as Marilyn prepared him for his morning bath.

Time outside of time ceased when the doctor drew a chair up beside me. He spoke, "It's polio, Dorothy. The spinal fluid is loaded with polio virus. We must find a place for you in a Buffalo hospital immediately, but I'll have to locate an ambulance first."

I tried to think. What about Peter and Danny? And Jack. He'd kissed me full on the lips Thursday night. Marilyn, who had been taking care of me and the boys, what about her? I had held Danny this morning to give him his six o'clock bottle. Peter had kissed me goodnight last night, and he snuggled beside me on the divan every so often.

Dear God! My mind bolted. It ran in one direction and then another, like a colt trying to find a weak place in the fence.

Would all these...these dear ones...have it, too?

The doctor was talking to me. "I think we ought to send Lloyd a cablegram. You be thinking about it while I call for an ambulance." He disappeared toward the telephone.

Lillian came up onto the side porch. She stopped when she reached the doorway to the living room. "We'll take care of Peter and Danny. Don't worry about them, Dottie." But her face...

Bad news travels fast.

The doctor reappeared. "Hello, Lillian. Did they tell you?" She nodded. "We've *got* to get her to a hospital immediately."

What he meant was—"out of this house, out of this town, away from all of the people she may contaminate with every extra minute she's here." But he didn't say that.

What he did say next caught me off guard, "I can't get an ambulance in Forestville. Everyone is afraid they'll be boycotted if it is known they carried polio. It could put them out of business. I'll try to find one in Silver Creek where no one will know the ambulance carried you. I'm sorry, but I can understand the problem."

Turning to me with forced cheerfulness, he said, "What shall we say in the cable?"

"How bad *is* the polio?"

He hedged, "I think it would be better to tell Lloyd it's a light case." He didn't look at me. "He's a long way from home, and he's in a dangerous line of work," he finished lamely.

I said, "*Is* it a light case?"

Patiently, as though speaking to a child, he tried to vindicate his judgment. My mind was fuzzy with pain and medication, but I clung tenaciously to the fact that Lloyd and I had never lied to each other.

Finally I said, "Doctor, if you send that message, you will have to sign it. I can't."

Near noon I was deposited on a stretcher and rolled out to the ambulance. Lillian was in the doorway with two-year-old Peter standing by her side. She had eight-month-old Danny in her arms. Her eyes were bright with unshed tears.

I wondered when I would see them again. I

wondered if Lloyd would get the cablegram today. I didn't know that at that very moment he was on the continent of Europe, a glider pilot in the Arnheim Invasion—A Bridge Too Far.

The ambulance door closed, shutting the sunshine out. No one could sit beside me. I was contaminated. As we pulled out of the driveway, I tried to raise up so I could see the little group on the steps one more time. My body wouldn't cooperate. I lay back down and closed my eyes. Each wave of pain was pursued by another.

The siren whined as the ambulance raced through the countryside. Grapes hung ripe on the vines. Corn was being cut for silage. The sun bathed the September afternoon with golden haze. September 23, 1944. I wondered on what date I would return—if I returned.

Awe-inspiring pain tore through my body. I was no longer aware of the countryside.

Lillian had called Daddy. He was at the hospital when I arrived, but I didn't know it. I was untouchable. The ambulance doors were sealed until hospital attendants and nurses gowned, masked and gloved, came to transfer me into the polio pavilion of the Millard Fillmore Hospital. I was sped into a private room. An iron lung was stationed in the hall outside my door.

When it was dusk, I thought I heard my name. Then I was sure I heard it. I couldn't raise myself very well, but I turned my head toward the window. In the gathering shadows Daddy stood. He was waving to me. Strength and courage flowed from him into me.

Circles of thought rolled and twisted themselves out of shape. Where had I heard it? Who had said to me, "All things work together for good...to them who love God." Daddy. Daddy had said it all my life. "We *know!*"

Polio and Peter and Danny and Lloyd and me—God could weave this into our lives for benefit. Well, *only* God could do that.

Four times a day I had Kenny packs. When the hot, moist packs were fastened around my legs, thighs, and back, there was a moment of no sensible pain. The heat drowned the pain, but only momentarily. It was pain such as I had never before experienced: arrogant, demanding, unending, never-diminishing. One aspirin and one codeine pill every four hours hardly touched the first layer of torment.

I thought back to the night in Bagley when I'd had appendicitis. I remembered the twenty-plus hours of hard labor when Peter was born. Those were sand-lot engagements. This was the big league. No breathing spells broke it up, no cessation at all.

I was paralyzed to my waist. My back and neck were weak, but they weren't painful. My arms hung like dead fish. All of the abdominal organs had been affected. My plumbing didn't work.

I wasn't sure what my condition was compared to that of others. I knew only that I was alone and scared. "Dear Father," I prayed. "You know about me. You knew this was going to happen, didn't You? Nothing surprises You, does it? But You're the only one who does know what's going to happen. The doctors don't know much about polio. And You're here. Give me the courage I need. Your promises are as good in the hospital as outside. Help me."

At mid-morning each day, a different group of neophyte doctors came into the room with the staff physician. They applied buzzers to my ankles and elbows to observe reflexes. They each grasped my hand to check my mushy grip. They said, "H'm," and like ghosts, they filed out.

I longed for the times for hot packs. The relief they brought was breathtaking. They masked the pain, but best of all, I had someone to talk to for fifteen minutes.

I averaged about an hour of sleep in each twenty-four hour period according to my night nurse. Having her there during the nights gave my churning thoughts an outlet. She stayed right in the room with me.

I couldn't have my Bible; I would contaminate it. So I remembered verses. I dredged them up out of the subconscious and clung to them.

I had never realized how weary I could become of myself. I was sick of my own thoughts. They were tired of me. But as tired as I was, there was no sleep. I remembered the psalm "for so He giveth His beloved sleep."[1] Now I knew why sleep was "beloved"; it provided surcease from self.

I thought about Lloyd, wondering where he was. I ruminated over the cable the doctor had sent. Had he gotten it? Would he come? And the boys, were they all right? Would they know me? I knew now I wasn't going to die.

On the morning of the eighth day, I heard a familiar laugh roll down the corridor. It was Dr. Stedem, our obstetrician. As he neared my door, his voice boomed, "Oh, now Nurse, we're not going to go through that again are we? Nobody knows how you get the stuff anyway. Frankly, I doubt whether one layer of white cheese cloth would impress the virus. If I'm gonna get it, I'll get it, and so will you! If not, so be it." With that he burst into the room looking like a human being.

Wearing a dark business suit, he was the apex of a cone of warmth and confidence that spread out behind him in a white world. I loved him.

"Are they taking good care of you, Dorothy?" he asked.

"Yes, pretty much," I said, "but tell me, how long is the pain going to last? The spasms, I mean."

He restrained his exuberance quickly. "I can't tell you. The maximum time is fourteen days. How long have you had them?"

"Over a week. Eight days. I can't sleep. D'you suppose I could have just one hypo so I could rest?" I knew I was begging. "There isn't much left to fight with."

"No. We can't give you a hypo," he said with regret but with finality. The heartiness had gone out of him. "Morphine is a nerve depressant," he went on. "If we put you out, even for a few minutes, that might be all it would take to prevent your walking for the rest of your life. The pain you have is proof that your muscles are still alive and fighting."

"That makes tons of difference!" I said breathlessly. "To know that, I mean. I can handle it now."

Only six more days and nights of pain, he had promised. I could bear that. My attitude did a 180° turn. If I just keep on hurting, I'll be okay. Now I wanted to hurt. I was afraid I wouldn't. It was incredible how the information changed everything.

The pain still rose in ceaseless waves, but I was over the hump. Six days left...five...four, no letup. Would it really stop, just like that? Three days. Was even this pain part of the 'all things'?

Two...one.

And then, like a curtain lifting, the pain was gone.

The next day the head nurse came into my room. She no longer wore the sterile gloves, gown, and mask. "Would you like to move into a semiprivate room?" she asked.

"Would I? Wow!"

When she went out, she left the door open. I had rejoined the human race. Within an hour I was moved. I had a roommate.

I couldn't be weighed because I couldn't stand, but my weight loss was estimated at fifty pounds.

Now that the contagion was past, Daddy was permitted to visit me every day. He brought me a radio and my Bible.

But I wanted Lloyd too. Surely he must have

received word by now. There was nothing from him.

"Dear God, bring him home. Now." It wasn't much of a prayer. It was a demand. Although I couched it in a polite tone of voice, it was still a demand. The children needed him desperately. Lillian couldn't take care of them much longer. As a pastor's wife and mother of three, she didn't need two more.

The indefiniteness of my recovery made planning difficult. Who would care for the boys? We needed Lloyd.

I was feverish in my disquietude for them. What would this do to them—being handed around as they surely would be. What could I do? God knew about this too, and He had allowed it. I had to settle for that.

My dependence on people irked me. I had been a do-it-yourself kit for too many years not to feel the distaste of being dependent. If I wanted anything that was five inches beyond my reach, I had to wait until someone happened in, or call for a nurse to expend her energy just to hand me what I thought I needed. It galled me.

I had cried "Why?" at Don's death. Now my own impotence stung me into asking it again.

Was I going to be a wheelchair dweller for the rest of my life? If I were, I wouldn't be the only sufferer—Lloyd and the boys would be victimized by it. What a repulsive thought!

My prayer for Lloyd's return began to change, gradually, imperceptibly. Perhaps he shouldn't see me like this. Maybe God was waiting until I had started on the road back before He would bring him. If so, that was a kindness.

I read and reread the Word, but I kept returning to Romans 8:28. I harbored a paradoxical idea: by the end of eternity (!) would I understand it all? Sometimes the verse seemed trite because it was so simple; other times I was confused by the whole of its implications. I kept finding things I hadn't seen before, sometimes because I hadn't wanted to.

"To them that are the called according to His purpose." That was the way the verse ended. According to *His* purpose. My purposes had been upset, horribly. The sickness, the pain, the loneliness, the uprooting of the babies! Hadn't God's purposes been upset *at all* by my misfortunes? Weren't God's purposes *ever* upset?

If they weren't, shouldn't my need for Lloyd make my love for God stronger? It didn't always. I wanted to manipulate God's plans and purposes so they would fit mine. I wanted Lloyd to be there.

If God brought Lloyd back safe and sound, could it be said that He had answered my prayer and Moth's by letting me have polio? Wow! Was I paying the bill for that prayer?

I searched my heart. Would I have been willing to pay this much had I been asked? A tentative "Yes" came through and grew stronger as I thought about it. Even if I were to live the rest of my life in a wheelchair, even then, how much better men the boys would become if they had a father to guide them.

Daddy often said, "Everything is on schedule with God." Could that really be so? The pain and the aloneness was still too fresh...too close...too real for me to believe that, but I wished I could.

If I didn't believe Him, was I calling Him a liar again?

I reached over my head to the bed post, grasped it firmly, and twisted my body so that my hips and legs would flop over. It was the only way I could turn. I was trying to duck the problem by doing something, anything within my limited range. Lloyd's presence was what I wanted most. I had suffered enough. I deserved to have him, didn't I?

What self-interest. Self-indulgence. Self-importance. What meanness! I wanted him there so he could see me suffer. God! What a rat I was!

I wept at the picture of myself. It was vivid. Then I cried, "God, forgive me. Don't bring him home until You want him here."

# CHAPTER
## SEVEN

## Rebuilding

Reading Catherine Marshall's Book, *A Man Called Peter,* I was convicted. I prayed the prayer of relinquishment and from that moment on I stopped jumping at every footstep in the corridor. I dumped the problem on the Lord. It changed everything. The longer the Lord kept him away, the better I would be when he came.

The Kenny packs continued, not to prevent injury, but to keep my legs limber for re-education.

The very day the spasms ceased, shortly after I had been moved to the semi-private room, a physiotherapist arrived. She 'carted' me down to the P-T room the next day. They were going to see what could be done with the leavings.

Infrared lamps warmed the muscles; finger-tip massage was applied; then came exercise. Guiding my legs in movement, the P-T people picked them up carefully, holding each leg firmly by the knee and ankle joint. Since there was no muscle to protect the bone, they could handle them no other way. The muscles had been detached from the bone. They slopped around in the skin so the leg reminded me of a pelican's pouch.

The physiotherapist explained that the myelin sheath, that iridescent envelope that surrounds and groups muscles, had been destroyed.

I had been anticipating therapy, knowing it was the path back to some kind of normalcy. I did not understand that it was going to be painful. The extreme pain that resulted from the therapist's bending my legs at the knee and hip took me by surprise. I realized that the re-education of the muscles was going to be accomplished only through hours on "the rack."

I couldn't give up. The easy course would be to call it quits and succumb to a wheel chair. A wheel chair was *no* solution; it presented another problem. I didn't believe God intended me to "wheel chair" my way through the rest of my life.

God, in His omniscience, knew which I would choose. He knows me better than I know myself. Therefore the pain that lay ahead must be part of God's plan for me. *How* I accepted the pain was up to me. I could rebel against it, I could accept it grudgingly or I could look past the pain to the hoped-for result of walking some day and again be thankful for pain. Pain despoils one of emotional energy. It is exhausting. I could hardly anticipate it with joy, not being a masochist. But again, I decided to let God carry the problem.

The exercise therapy consisted of lifting a leg one inch, bending at the knee and hip. Rest. Recover. Lift an inch and a quarter. Return. Rest. And so on. The same torment accompanied every fraction of an inch. Fortunately the doctors at Millard Fillmore and the therapists were of the school that raised a limb to the point of pain, not beyond as others did.

I recognized the necessity of thinking muscle movement. But such movement is involuntary, not

consciously willed. I could not dredge up in my
mind the memory of the sensation of muscle movement. It had been erased from my memory bank.

My college training in physical education was
an advantage. Maybe that was why God had me
change my major in college — He knew I'd need
it. Daddy brought my anatomy book in from home.
I went to work re-learning muscle origin and insertion. No classroom test could compare with my
now desperate need to help in the retraining. The
doctors who worked with me said that my being
able to picture muscle origin and insertion positive-
ly affected my recovery.

Thankfulness welled up in me. How grateful I
was that I, rather than Peter or Danny, had been
stricken. As an adult, I had a greater possibility
of maximum recovery than a child would for two
reasons. My muscles were fully grown at the onset
of the disease, and as an adult, I could direct con-
scious thought in the re-education of the muscles.

One day, when I felt I had made good progress
on the road back, Lillian and Paul obtained permission to bring Pete and Danny to see me. What a
bonus! I was hungry to lay eyes on them.

It's hard to say what frightened them. Was it
the strangeness — the all-whiteness — of the
hospital? Could it have been the uncertainty in
their lives for the past weeks? I don't know. They
looked wonderfully healthy as they came through
the door. Paul placed Pete on the bed beside me.
I put my arms out to draw him close. He pulled
away with fear in his eyes and no recognition. He

began to cry. Danny joined in. They howled. The visit was short.

After they had gone, I lay staring out the window with unseeing eyes. What had turned this lovely idea into a fiasco? I picked up a mirror and looked at myself. I saw huge eyes in a skin-and-bones face, unpretty hair, a warmed-over skeleton.

What was I supposed to learn from this? How it felt to be rejected by my own children? What it's like to be good for nothing? Add this to my complete loathing of dependency. Pile on top my need for Lloyd and my distress at the total silence from him. Finish it off with the colossal question mark that hovered over the likelihood of my ever walking again. Just what *was* I supposed to learn? The thankfulness departed.

Once more I thought of Job. I reached for my Bible and writhed with him through his agony in a brand new way. The big thing seemed to be the difference between God's view of the situation and man's view. Several principles surfaced. One: Satan could not hurt Job without God's permission. Two: God would never permit the hurt without a reason. Three: God knew Job's spiritual condition and would not have entrusted him with such tragedies if there had been doubt of the outcome. Four: Uncounted millions of believers down through time have been heartened and lifted over the rough spots because of Job's suffering. Five: Job's difficulties, then, were "chosen" by God with love and care; Job's responses became gifts to the human race — certainly one of the reasons why

God allowed them. Six: My difficulties, then, are
"gifts" carefully chosen by a loving Father to elicit
responses that will glorify Him. Seven: I'd better
get busy and be thankful and remember what I promised God back in 1932.

I had made a blanket commitment then. Now
I must make a specific commitment, without which
the first commitment was meaningless. Everything
*was* on schedule with God.

One Saturday morning I was propped up in bed
knitting a suit for Peter. The head nurse came to
the door and said, "Are you ready for a visitor?"
She paused as she turned to go and said, "It's not
your dad, but it *is* someone you'd awfully like to
see."

Lloyd stood in the doorway! There he was, all
khaki and dirty and wonderful. My breath stuck in
my windpipe, "No! No! No!" I finally choked. What
I meant was "Yes! Yes! Yes!" I don't know why I
said "No." He was too good to believe.

He held me close. His strong shoulders shook
from weariness and relief. It had been eight
months. No words at first. Neither of us could trust
our voices. Finally he said, "You'll never believe
how I happen to be here."

I devoured him with my eyes.

"We left from Stone, England, and went to
Prestwick, Scotland. We stopped at the Azores.
Newfoundland was next. We were supposed to land
at La Guardia, but we couldn't. It was weathered
in. Next alternative — Presque Isle, Maine. More
bad weather. Third: Buffalo! And here I am."

He was all there. Whole. I was speechless.

He went on, "As soon as I learned we were to land in Buffalo, I told the captain about you and my reason for coming home. He called Fort Totten to see if he could leave me in Buffalo."

"Really?" I had found my voice, "What'd they say?"

"Negative! Proceed to destination. Y'see, I'm not legally in the United States yet."

"How come you're here then?"

"I stayed aboard after all the other men piled out to get milkshakes and hamburgers for the first time in eight months. The captain came down the aisle and said, "How long does it take to get to the hospital?' I told him about half an hour. He said, 'We'll be grounded here two hours. Get going!' "

He could stay half an hour. He called Forestville. His little 70-year-old Norwegian mother had come from Wisconsin and was at our house taking care of the boys. Then he called Daddy and Mother.

After being revived from the shock of looking at my legs, he struggled out of his khaki sweater and draped it over the bedpost. "There," he said, "if you think this was all a dream, reach over and feel my sweater."

It was time to go. "I hope that taxi is right where I left it," he said, and he was gone.

I lay still a long time remembering the hour six days before when I had prayed the prayer of relinquishment.

Twenty-four hours after he reached headquarters, he was granted leave. He marched into my room again.

"Hold it! Hold it!" he said, anticipating all of my questions, "First, I have a month's leave, but I don't know how long before I'll be out permanently."

"Then the war is over for you?"

"It looks that way."

"Oh, dear God, I'm *so* thankful. No one knows *how* thankful I am."

"You're not including me in that 'no one' category, I hope."

He recounted his experiences the night he flew back from the invasion. Glider pilots were as expendable as their gliders. They had to hitch rides out of the battle zone and out of the country. Sixty-five percent of the glider pilots had been killed in that engagement. God's hand had been on him.

He said that when he found the cablegram on his bed and read it, it sounded like doubletalk. The thought of polio brought dismay, but the cablegram said a "light case." What did that mean? That very untruth prevented him from flying home for over a month.

He had received no word for twenty-nine days after the cablegram. The fall military push was on. Nothing but vitally needed supplies, men, and ordnance were shipped across the Atlantic. Personal mail going either way was non-essential. He didn't know I might never walk again. The muzzle on the mail nearly drove him out of his mind.

After riding co-pilot for weeks on daily C-47

supply missions into Holland, he applied for leave. Other surviving glider pilots had been allowed a week's leave to rest and recover, but Lloyd had stayed on the base trying to find a way to get back to the States. Every possibility had been blocked. Perhaps if he went to London, he could find his cousin, Col. Andy Ofsthun, a Command Pilot.

He found Andy and told him the problem.

Andy said, "Who's your C.O.?"

"Col. Fox is Chief of Staff of the 9th Troop Carrier Command."

"Jimmy Fox?"

"Yep, Col. Jimmy Fox. Why, do you know him?"

"Went to West Point with him. Hand me the phone."

Lloyd turned to me and said, "That was five days ago, and here I am checked in at Fort Totten and checked out to you."

When he got to Forestville, he found that the care of Pete and Danny was too much for Mother Galde. A few days later he took Pete to Milwaukee to live with my brother Mason and his wife Dottie and their two boys. Lloyd's brother Cliff and his wife Frieda in Duluth took Danny. Danny learned to walk and talk within Frieda's care, not mine.

I set my jaw harder than ever toward the goal of gaining strength.

When Lloyd's month was gone, he went to Fort Dix to be reassigned to Stateside duty. He would be speaking at war plants that had earned the "E" for excellence.

I still couldn't raise my legs from the bed. Perhaps if I had known that I never would be able to, I might not have had the courage to keep trying. Today, if I strain too much trying to push my legs around in bed by themselves, charley horse takes over. Often I have to take midnight baths to relax the muscles sufficiently to reinvite sleep.

One day two of the nurses slid me off the side of the bed, and I stood on my own feet. I stood because one bone was stacked on another. I had to extend the knees backward to keep my legs from buckling. Even now I don't have enough muscle to hold up the weight of my body.

By means of intense concentration and the assistance of two people, I started to walk. No part of the walking was involuntary. Danny would begin his walking by creeping and crawling; I would begin mine by walking with people. Two things Danny had in his favor: he didn't have so far to fall, and he had more cushion.

Because of muscle damage, I couldn't sit up without bracing myself with my arms or by leaning against a solid object. I tried once and would have gone headfirst onto the floor if a nurse hadn't caught me. Panting from exertion, she planted me back in bed, arranged the sandbag to hold my feet in position, and marched out.

The sandbag was uncomfortable. It required my staying in one place while the bag held my feet at right angles to my legs. Without it, the feet flopped forward so that the toes almost touched the bed. This creates a dropped foot, often corrected with surgery. If I had not disciplined myself to sleep with the sandbag in place, and to have it there most of the day, I would have ended up with dropped feet.

One day a P-T nurse came for me. She was all smiles.

"Guess what! You get promoted today," she said.

"To what?" I knew it must be good, but I was cautious.

"To the hydrotherapy room!" she said on our way to the elevator.

After the infrared treatment and light massage, she came for me again. "Here's our new water baby," she said.

In diaper and hospital gown, I was laid gently in a sheet sling in a tub of warm water. The soothing flow around me put me to sleep.

In a couple of weeks, I graduated to a stainless steel tank. It looked like a horse trailer wrapped in silver satin. In it there was a cloth sling to sit on. The water was not moving when they hoisted my spindly legs over the edge of the tank. The nurse moved around to the front of the machine. "Contact! Ready for the takeoff?" she said as she placed the hand on a lever.

"Roger." I held on to the sides.

Air jetted through the water with forceful pressure, more than my legs had yet encountered. It hurt good.

From that day I made progress so fast it was hard to believe. My legs grew noticeably stronger, although the right quadriceps muscle that raises the leg was dead. The tailor muscle that cuts kitty-corner from the outside of the thigh to the inside of the knee was rather strong. It threw my leg oddly when I tried to walk. The strong tendons (or hamstrings) underneath the knee were gone on the right, but faintly present on the left leg. The calf muscle pulled the leg up quite well on both sides. I had almost no long muscles on the insides of the upper leg. Without them, no one can stand up on ice; the splits come uninvited. The long muscles, or abductors, lift the leg sideways. Mine were fair.

When Lloyd came back in a few weeks, we had a new set of problems. Our insurance had been used up. I still had months of hospital care ahead of me.

One afternoon a charming lady walked into the room. She was a stranger to us, but as she talked, it was apparent that we were not strangers to her.

"You have two little boys," she said with interest. "And you've been in the hospital since the twenty-ninth of September, haven't you, Mrs. Galde? You're making an excellent recovery for a polio patient."

"I hope so," I said. "I'm trying hard."

"Yes, you are," she agreed. She was standing at the foot of the bed. "I'm from the National Foundation for Infantile Paralysis. Our motto is: 'No one can afford polio.' You are not to worry about the financial part of this battle. Millions of Americans are ready to help with that. You just keep on working as you have. We're proud of you."

"Thank you!" Happiness always makes me
weak, but my waterworks didn't rev up until she
was gone. I hadn't realized that The March of
Dimes would affect us personally when I had put
my dimes in.

I wanted to try to walk alone. I had something
in the back of my head that I hadn't yet dared put
into words. One afternoon late in November, Miss
Longo, the head nurse came into my room after
I'd wakened from my nap. I was making sock dolls
for Christmas presents.

"Are you ready for the great experiment?" she
asked. She had another nurse in tow.

"What? Oh! I know. I'm going to walk by myself. Yes. Shut the door. Sink or swim, let's have
it be private," I said as I threw off the covers.

Between the two nurses, I stood beside the bed,
properly stacked. I was propped up against the bed.
They backed up, about three feet away. I was con-
centrating with every ounce. Knees hyper-
extended, my exchange of weight from one leg to
the other was carefully accomplished. I was walking as would a man on stilts, although with less
confidence. One step. Another. A third. I was
there, hanging onto Miss Longo. I had done it.

They helped me back into bed. I was flushed
with victory. I wanted to try it again, instantly.

"No. That's enough for one day, and don't even
*think* of trying it when we're not here. Got that?"

I made no promises.

Several days later, after walking a few steps every afternoon, it seemed time to try a turn-around. Three steps back to my bed.

I made the initial three steps to Miss Longo. She helped me turn around and held me while I launched myself for the return trip. Stiff-legged, feeling like a young ostrich, I started back. Some of that 100% concentration had bled off in the excitement. Whatever it was, that hair-breadth difference was all that catastrophe required. I fell to the terrazzo floor like a bag of rocks. The nurses picked me up gently and inserted me between cool sheets.

How could I ever walk if it was going to hurt *that* much? I burrowed under my pillow and gave in to self-pity, but it was disappointment too, and most of all physical hurt.

From that time, I had to fight the fear of falling in addition to maintaining maximum concentration. Deep purple bruises decorated my body regularly. Why I didn't break something, I don't know.

It would have been easier to stay in bed.

After Daddy heard the story of my falls, he put his mind to the problem. That same ingenuity had perfected the windshield wiper, the two little squirts, and push-button windows. My father had five hundred other inventions on record at the Patent Office in Washington. Now he concocted an adult-size U-shaped walker. I was helped in from behind. The upper bars came about two inches beneath my armpits, not supporting me, but there to catch me when I fell. A second bar at finger-tip height helped me to propel the walker. Ball bearing rollers made it easy to manipulate. Now I had sore armpits instead of everything else — a nice change.

I ventured into the hall without breaking into a cold sweat. If I wandered too far and became tired, a nurse helped lift my feet to the bottom bars; then she rolled me back to my room.

Tiredness came upon me like the dropping of a curtain. There was no such thing as "getting tired." It happened all at once. No preparation for the fatigue was possible. One minute I'd feel great; the next I collapsed. It was many years before this pattern disappeared.

What I wanted most was to walk at Christmas. Lloyd had never seen me take a step without help. He didn't know about the falls and bruises. I kept them covered. The fact that he was away for weeks at a time on speaking tours is probably the only reason I succeeded in keeping my secret. I'm terrible about keeping secrets, but I kept this one. I *was* going to walk by myself at Christmas.

The holidays were less than a month away when the hospital authorities agreed to let me go home for the holidays. It was to be for only three days, but that sounded like a month. Lloyd came for me. He carried me to the car from the wheelchair and then folded it up to take with us.

"Let's go home by the lake road," I suggested as we pulled away from the hospital. "My horizon has been so limited lately, I need to see a broad sweep of sky."

When we drove into Hamburg on Lake Street, Lloyd turned up Pleasant Avenue.

"Oh! Good. We'll go past the skating rink," I said.

"I thought you'd like that."

He slowed down as we came to the high school. On the left, across the street from the high school, was the practice field about an acre in size. The field had been cleared of snow, and the snow had been piled around the perimeter into banks that would hold water. The firemen hitched up big hoses to flood the field. How many nights I had skated there! Ice skating was my favorite winter sport.

I watched the graceful movement on the rink. Figure skaters, couples in close formation, little kids with wobbly ankles in spite of double runners, speed skaters lengthening stride, the special sound of blades scraping on ice. It was all there.

I rolled up my window and turned away.

Never again would I be a whole person. Would I ever be able to suppress the envy in my heart? It was one more emotion that God called sin, and I must deal with it.

After dinner on Christmas Day, we all sat around the tree. As the presents were opened, wrappings were stuffed into baskets. Finally the last present had been opened. Before the group could disintegrate, I cleared my throat and made my announcement.

"I have one more present," I said. Everyone turned toward me. I made a visual sweep of the floor to see if anything had been left that might trip me. Lloyd was too close, Daddy was across the circle.

Placing my hands solidly on the arms of my chair, and remembering all the things I had learned in hours of practicing how to arise from a chair, I stood.

I didn't dare look at anyone for fear of breaking my concentration. I braced my knees back as far as they would go. Awkwardly I transferred the weight from one leg to the other, and I walked five steps toward Daddy, a hesitant, tentative turn around, and five steps back to Lloyd.

He had risen, astonished. Nobody could speak. He caught me in his arms. When I was safe there, I closed my eyes. I could smell the fragrance of the Christmas tree, the wood smell from the fireplace, the Old Spice from Lloyd.

I could feel the loveliness of home around us, the wide windows letting in the sun-sparkled snow scene, the tall ceiling giving stateliness to the picture. Most of my Christmases had been celebrated in this room. It was very dear to me.

My heart was near to bursting with joy, and everybody was crying. I had kept my secret too well, I guess.

I raised my head from Lloyd's shoulder and said, "What's all the honking about? Sounds like a flock of geese on their way south."

I had to sit down before my legs gave out. With all the hugs and kisses and joy flowing unhindered, I was better off in the safety of a chair.

The next day I went back to the hospital for two more months.

## The Fire

In January and February, Lloyd spent several hours a day at the hospital learning the correct method of massage and the way to manage my legs during the exercises. I was still in a critical period.

I had to be extremely careful not to overdo. The process of recuperation must not be hurried. I had been in the hospital nearly half a year, but I could go home too soon. I would not be considered well for two years, but during that time I would work to re-educate and strengthen the muscles that had been affected.

As my days in the hospital came to an end, I realized as I probably hadn't before that I now talked with the Lord more easily than with people. I started conversations the moment I opened my eyes and continued throughout the day. When I needed to hear Him, I would search for more promises in the Scripture. I fed on them.

It is true that man does not live by bread alone, but by every word that proceeds out of the mouth of God.[1] "Lord, keep me close," I prayed. "When I get back to normal life, will I be able to talk to You all the time the way I have here?"

As eager as I was to head for home, I was loathe to vacate a nearness to God I had not felt before. I knew that He wouldn't move away, but that I might.

We spent a month in Hamburg with Mother
and Daddy before we moved back to Forestville to
run our own household. Lloyd had been given an
honorable discharge and mustered out on the
grounds of hardship.

Before we left Hamburg, Lloyd went to Milwaukee to reclaim Peter. He was now two and a
half. I wondered if he would remember me. It
wasn't easy waiting for them to come. I conjured
up tableaux in my mind that were not comforting.
I could see him not wanting to leave Uncle Mason
to go with a daddy he hardly knew. I remembered
the afternoon in the hospital. The burn in my mind
from that day had never really healed. I was afraid.

I dressed carefully. I sat watching the street.
When I saw them drive in, I couldn't move. What
little strength I had ran out like water.

They came in by the side porch, Peter holding
Lloyd's hand as they opened the door. A flicker of
uncertainty passed over his face as he reluctantly
let go of his daddy's hand. Then, turning full toward
me, he held out his arms and ran into mine. "Hello,
Mama," he said.

"Hello, darling!" It was joy absolute to feel the
warmth of his little body pressed against mine.

Above his small head, my eyes met Lloyd's. He
had prepared Peter for this meeting. I knew it. He
made sure it would be a satisfying meeting.

Love is infectious. "Mama, this is our real family, isn't it?" Peter chattered happily as he played
with his cars on the floor. "We aren't going to go

away any more at all, are we? When can we get
Danny?" He was saying all the things I was
thinking.

On the first of March we returned to Forestville,
back to the same house. To the funny little doorway at the head of the stairs; Peter appropriated
that immediately. To Dr. Hutchinson's bunk bed;
Peter and I had taken naps on it when Lloyd was
overseas. To lilac bushes showing tight buds in an
early spring. Lloyd carried me into the house.
Lillian and Paul were there. She had cleaned the
house. Flowers were on the table.

Lloyd was home, I was home, and so was Peter.
Three down and one to go. Peter's eyes sparkled
as he followed my every move. Marilyn was helping us again so I would not do too much. I was
coming alive all over again. Each time I felt Peter's
soft arms around my neck, the love that had been
pinched off for months poured through me more
strongly than ever. When would Danny come?

The only things I learned about Lloyd's experiences in Holland were overheard. One evening as Lillian and I were finished with the dishes
from a late snack of cola and brunschwager sand-
wiches, we overheard Lloyd recounting his return
down the "corridor" from Holland to the city of
Brussels after his flight into Nijmegen. Moving into the room quietly, we sat down, resumed our
mending, and listened.

"There were a thousand gliders in our sky
train," Lloyd said. "It took two hours for the entire

train to pass a given point."

"Did you absorb much flak on your way in?" Paul asked.

"Some. I sat on my flak suit, figuring it would be coming up from below. Two planes in front of us were shot down. One glider beside me went. The hedges, ditches, and rows of Lombardy poplar were more of a problem than the flak for those of us in the lead squadron. They were closer together than those in the fields of England or at Lumberton, North Carolina, where we trained. I was fortunate to be up front. Some of the boys coming in afterward couldn't find a spot to land."

"What did they do, for heaven's sake?"

"Crashed in mid-air trying to get into fields that were too small. Some of them sliced through others before the guys could get out. Others broke apart in the air and spilled men, jeeps, high explosives — everything they carried — onto the scramble below. Some of the gliders veered too far east and landed in Germany. It was a fiasco," he said, shuddering.

"Where were you when all this happened?"

"In a ditch. We crawled down into one of the deep ditches that surround each farmer's land. We kept crawling until we came to a crossroads. Then a farmer came out of his barn on the other side of the road, and we waved to him. He sauntered over casually, trying not to attract attention."

"Were you able to talk with him?"

"Not a one of us knew the language, but he knew we were Americans. He motioned us to follow him to his barn, and he brought us fresh milk, cheese, and homemade bread from the house. I'd never tasted anything so heavenly in all my life."

"Weren't you in danger?" Paul asked.

"Were we! Right smack in the middle of it. During the night we heard tanks or trucks moving up the road. We didn't know whether they were English or German. I took my boots off before I fell asleep in the hay. Nobody else did, but I figured I could run faster in my bare feet anyway."

"Were they still moving in the morning?"

"No, the road was clear. We walked down it several miles. The troops with us left to mine their objective, a bridge across the Maas River. We reconnoitered until we found a command post. The colonel in charge told us we could wait around until they got a convoy ready to go down the corridor. The boys were restless. They didn't want to wait."

"What else could you do?"

"Across the road there were a couple of American red-ball trucks. The drivers were waiting to be told what to do, so I told 'em. I gave the order to move out for Brussels. I was the only second lieutenant in the bunch; the rest were flight officers. We piled onto the trucks and took off.

"Half the way down the corridor, we went around the square in one little town. I wasn't paying attention. The driver chose a road and had gone about two miles when it struck us that it was too quiet. We banged on the top of the cab and told him to turn around. When we got back to the town, we found we'd been heading straight into Germany.

The Lord sure was looking after us."

"Close!" muttered Paul.

"Another place, we saw German Panzers cross-ing the corridor. They were high-tailing it back to Germany. We stopped, ran into an abandoned house, and turned to see one of our glider pilots unhook a grenade from his belt, pull the pin, and toss a high fast-ball into the middle of one of those babies. It blew sky high."

"Was he nuts?"

"I guess so. You had to be a little nuts to sur-vive in gliders. They must've been in a whopping hurry, or we'd have all been dead. One panzer turned its snout toward us, lobbed one in our direc-tion and wiped out our front truck. Then he shifted his course back to the run for Germany and kept on going. We finally made it to Brussels and spent the night between linen sheets in a ritzy hotel."

"How long did you stay in Brussels?"

"Some of the guys caught rides to Paris and stayed a couple of weeks after they'd picked up their pay. In my squadron of twelve glider pilots, three of us were left. We learned later that the Ger-mans killed 6000 of the 8000 Britishers who land-ed on the north bank of the Rhine. They didn't even take 'em prisoners, just killed 'em." Lloyd shook his head at the thought.

"But you, what did you do?"

"I took a trolley out to the airport and sand-bagged in the first plane I could find heading back to England. You see, the next day was my birth-day. The Bottomleys, friends I had met in Sleaford, were planning a birthday party for me with sugar rations they had saved up for weeks. I couldn't let a birthday cake go to waste."

"Did you make it in time?"

"When I got to my barracks, I found the cablegram saying that Dottie had polio. I tried to find out more. Finally I went in to Sleaford to tell them. It wasn't much of a celebration. Weeks later with still no more news, I put in for combat fatigue leave. That was when I left for London and found my cousin Andy Ofsthun."

As I sat listening to Lloyd, I remembered the agreement Moth and I had made asking God to spare his life. God had used polio to bring him back when He did. I was satisfied that my crippled legs were not too much to pay for having him back. The boys would have their father. No price was too high for that.

In May the lilacs bloomed by the back door. I remembered the row of lilacs in Wheaton that had accompanied Don's courtship. I recalled the lilac bush by the front doorstep in Bagley. Don and I never saw that bush bloom. Now Lloyd's and my lilac bush was fragrant and full-bloomed.

The county nurse visited me weekly, and the first week of May I was summoned to the orthopedic clinic in Gowanda, a neighboring town. All of the polio victims in towns around Buffalo were to be evaluated. We were to have muscle grading and additional therapy prescribed. Paul and Lloyd took me. After waiting a couple of hours, I was admitted to the examination room.

One of the therapists graded my muscles. She handed the report to the orthopedic surgeon as he strode into the room. I lay on the table. He scanned the sheet with a frown creasing his forehead deeper and deeper. I knew I didn't have much to work with, but I wasn't prepared for him.

With a bellow, he said, "What in hell is she doing out of the hospital?" He hardly looked at me. "Is there any room for her at West Haverstraw?"

I knew where West Haverstraw was: on the Hudson, four hundred miles away.

The therapist, quite overawed, ventured a timid reply, "No, Doctor, that's for patients under twenty-one."

*Well, hooray for my side,* I thought.

"Is there any room at Ithaca?" he thundered.

"I don't know for sure, but I believe not. There's usually a long waiting list," she said.

I lay there absorbing the scene. I might as well have been a potted plant on the window sill. I thought, *Bless his heart; it hasn't occurred to him that I'm not going back to any hospital.*

He came over to me, still not seeing me, just a body. His bushy eyebrows met in a fierce frown as he barked, "Well, she'll have to have a full-length brace on the right leg. If she doesn't, she's going to have a curvature of the spine. That will bring on arthritis. One leg must be at least two inches shorter than the other. I'd like to know why they ever let her out of the hospital!"

Steam issued from his nostrils.

I could have told him why they let me out of

the hospital if he had asked. It was because the doctors and therapists at Millard Fillmore had hearts. They had taught Lloyd how to give me the therapy I needed. But he didn't want to know ... from me.

We ordered the brace and had to purchase special shoes at $25 a pair for it to be built on.

All of my medical encounters were not as galling as that one. Later in the month we went in to see the doctor who had supervised the polio pavilion at Millard Fillmore and my initial recovery.

When we entered the office, he was talking to his receptionist. His face lit up when he saw us.

"Come in! Come in!" he said. Then turning to the young woman behind the desk, he said, "Joan, may I introduce you to the lady who never should have walked, Mrs. Galde."

During our visit with him, he asked us as a favor to him to attend an orthopedic clinic to be held at Buffalo General Hospital the following week. He assured us that he would be there. His reason for wanting me to go was to substantiate statements he had made in a medical meeting about my recovery. His colleagues had refused to believe him.

We went. It was different from the other one. After the therapist had graded the muscles as before, she handed the sheet to the orthopedic surgeon who entered. He scrutinized it, his eyebrows rising and rising.

"Did you walk in here?" he asked me kindly.

"Yes, sir."

"May I see you walk?"

I slid off the examination table very carefully, maintaining my balance constantly. I gathered my concentration, then walked toward him.

He stood there, his chin in his hand, and looked at me in wonderment.

"Turn around and lift your gown, can you?"

In the ever-present diapers for these engagements, I turned slowly, with vigilance. I walked back to the table.

"What do you do it *with,* may I ask?"

My doctor grinned as the surgeon faced him and said, "You were right. I never would have believed it. Now I know that all of the soldiers didn't go overseas."

This was progress. A few days later, the brace arrived. Using it, I had to walk with a stiff leg, and that disturbed my system of balance. I had been taught to walk in a special way. When I fell now with a leg encased in metal, I fell from full height. It was far more damaging and painful. The five pounds of extra weight made it more exhausting to walk and harder to handle myself. I sounded like the anvil chorus when I hit the deck.

And I was pregnant.

Each afternoon, Marilyn came over to fix the evening meal for the three of us. Danny was still in Duluth. I was suffering the early pregnancy nausea four or five times a day. When Marilyn came on the afternoon of Decoration Day, I hobbled out to the side porch and crawled under the electric blanket. The fresh, sharp air revived me.

Lloyd came home from the machine shop down the street where he had found a job. Because the work was new and demanding, he was fatigued and ready for bed shortly after dinner.

We had hardly settled down when a little voice broke the silence, "Daddy, I need a drink."

Groaning, Lloyd struggled out of bed and went downstairs for a glass and water. He told Peter, firmly, to go to sleep.

As we dozed off, we heard toys hitting the floor. Lloyd rubbed his eyes and again went to Peter's bedroom. This time he used a persuasive touch for emphasis.

He crawled back into bed and we both fell asleep. Suddenly I awoke. I didn't know how long I had slept, but I heard things dropping again. *That little stinker!* I thought, but I didn't want to get Lloyd up. The dropping didn't stop. It was getting louder. Finally it wakened Lloyd. We sat up in bed at the same time. It was 1:30 AM.

As we looked toward Peter's room, we caught a glimpse of yellow leaping and falling. We could see through the open guest room door and the jumping yellow was outside the window where the bunk bed was.

Fire!

And we were on the second floor!

Lloyd bounded out of bed into instant speed and action. He raced through the door and down the stairs. His commando training had propelled him into immediate reconnaissance.

I knew by the way he had reacted that there

was no time to waste — surely no time for me to
struggle into that horrid brace. I had not walked
without shoes before, but I did then. My feet tingl-
ed as they touched the bare floor. The bony struc-
ture of my feet had little protection. It hurt each
time I put my foot down.

I had to hold onto the wall. No lights. I didn't
dare defy all of my walking rules, but there wasn't
time to be careful. As I reached the hall, the sounds
of dropping increased. It was the pictures being
burned off the living room wall downstairs.

I groped toward Peter's room. Grasping the
knob, I opened the door. Darkness. He was asleep.

Flames leaped and fell as they mounted the roof
outside his window. Geysers of sparks erupted with
burning wood as it flew upward.

I leaned over Pete's bed, bracing myself against
it. Bending down, I gathered him into my arms and
tried to rise. I couldn't. My back wouldn't straighten
up. He was too heavy. His sleep-weighted body
pulled me down so that I nearly lost my footing.
Oh God!

"Where are you?" Lloyd's voice was command-
ing, urgent, as he vaulted the stairs.

"In here!"

"Where?" he screamed.

"In Peter's room," I shouted.

In an instant he was beside me. "I'll take him,"
he said roughly. He was deciding beyond me.
There was no time to communicate. He wrapped
Peter in a blanket and they were gone.

Lloyd's rapid movement gave me a sense of

impending disaster, of utmost need for haste. My mouth was dry with fear. Suddenly, I knew I must save myself. There would not be time for Lloyd to come back for me.

I fell to the floor; that was the quickest way to get there. I must use the little door at the head of the stairs. Dragging my bad leg, I crept to the cubby-hole door. I thrust my head out into the stairway to see where the fire was. Woosh! The flames caught my hair. I backed up and swatted the fire out. I mustn't breathe. Scorching air would burn my breathing tubes; that kills, too. The stair-well had become a flue. Fire rushed upward, filling the upper half of the stairwell. I must stay low, beneath the flames.

The stairs were steep. Thanks, Lord. I pulled my legs around in front of me into the little opening. Before I pushed my legs out, I inhaled deeply in the dark of Peter's room. Then I squeezed through the little door into the flaming stairway.

I was encased in fire. *Move, move!* I thought, *Dear God, don't let Lloyd come for me. You get me out.*

I was sliding, falling, groping, tumbling through heat and yellow fire. I couldn't hold my breath much longer, but I was not down yet. I thrust my left hand out across my body to the door jamb on my right to steady myself. Then I fell the rest of the way. The floor scorched. Ahead of me flames rose to the ceiling. I pulled my body through the doorway of Loda's kitchen, dragging my right leg on the red-hot floor. Reaching back, I shoved my bad leg off the scalding floor.

Fear left me some place in my flight through the yellow tunnel. Peace settled over me.

"Thank God you're safe!" Lloyd said as he leaned over me. "How could you come down so fast? I waked Loda, put Peter on the front porch, and was coming back to get you, but you're here." I rested against him as he seized the phone to report the fire, and I breathed a prayer of thanksgiving that Danny had not yet come home.

Lloyd picked me up in his arms. I didn't feel the live coal on his shoulder burning my arm. Loda scooped Peter up; he was standing on the porch in his Dr. Dentons fast asleep. As we reached Pattyson's big front door, the living room windows behind us exploded. Flames gushed out greedily for oxygen and clawed up the side of the house.

By that time Pattyson's phone line had been burned through, so Lloyd ran down to Paul and Lillian's to call the doctor.

I put my hand on the baby within me. He was quiet. When Peter and Danny had been three months along, I had nearly miscarried. With this baby, the fall downstairs, the badly burned face and arm, not a flicker of difficulty. They took me to the hospital because a miscarriage was expected. They didn't know how badly burned I was until they got the black soot off my face.

Three weeks in the hospital elapsed before I stood with Lloyd beside the ruins of our first home. Nightmares had accompanied every night in the hospital. Every time, my subconscious mind work-

ed out another way to get out of a second story
when the first was aflame.

The burns on my face, my arms, my hands, my
neck were healing well. The boils and sties that had
erupted as a result of cooked flesh needing exit
were more comfortable now. The scar from the live
coal on Lloyd's shoulder had become a keloid that
would whiten in time.

Little had survived the fire. We left the black-
ened skeleton and turned back to Paul and Lillian's.
Low lying clouds engulfed the setting sun. We turned toward the trail by the creek. "This is the path
I learned by heart when you were overseas," I said.

"Put your arm across my shoulder so you won't
fall," Lloyd said as he steadied me on the uneven
ground. God had made Lloyd's shoulder just a few
inches above mine. We walked together comfor-
tably. I was glad he wasn't six feet tall.

"Look at the clouds with the sun behind them!"
I exclaimed. Beyond the laciness of the willows lay
a blaze of color. "Isn't that what can happen to our
clouds?"

"Stand still a minute so I can look up."

"If those clouds weren't up there, it wouldn't be
as good a sunset, would it?" I asked.

"I guess not," he mused. "I never thought about
that before. Without clouds, the sun just goes
down. It takes the clouds to reveal the beauty of
the sun. D'you think that's why God gives us hard
things? So we can reflect the beauty of the Son?"

"One reason, surely."

The shining gold and silver, the shafts of rose

and salmon, the silver-edged clouds made an imprint that has not been forgotten.

Was that what I had asked for that night in Wheaton? A heavenly connection between "Thy will be done" and "All things work together for good to them who love God, to them who are called according to His purpose" slipped into place.

Days etched in ice or snow or pain or fire. Death, heartbreak, work, tears, laughter, and love. Separation, polio, utter dependence, the yellow of sunshine and fire, scars, legs that would never walk right ... "All things."

# PART III

## THE REAPING: Romans 8:38 Trusted

*"Though he slay me, yet will I trust in him, I will maintain mine own ways before him." Job 13:15*

# Through It All

I've had many tears and sorrows
I've had questions for tommorow
There've been times I didn't know right from wrong
But in every situation
God gave blessed consolation
That my trials come to only make me strong.

I thank God for the mountains
And I thank Him for the valleys,
I thank Him for the storms
He brought me through
For if I'd never had a problem
I wouldn't know that He could solve them
I'd never know what faith in God could do.

Through it all,
Through it all,
I've learned to trust in Jesus,
I've learned to trust in God.
Through it all,
Through it all,
I've learned to depend on His Word.

*Andrae Crouch*

# CHAPTER
## NINE

## Memory Stones

The book of Joshua, chapters 3 and 4, gives a beautiful pattern—a "how-to-respond" format for the times when God moves in power in our lives. Joshua tells us that two million Israelites were stopped on the east side of the Jordan. It was the time of the barley harvest; snows from the mountains overflowed the river with icy, rushing water. On the west side was Jericho, the first and most difficult military objective in the conquest of Canaan. God set the stage (He often does) with a humanly impossible situation: The Israelites had to cross the raging river.

He said, "Move forward into the water." He had changed His method of leading the people of Israel, no longer using the cloud by day and fire by night. Now it was the Ark of the Covenant they were to follow. But God Himself had not changed. "Step into the flood, and the water will stop flowing," He said.

God does that to us, too. It takes faith. We either believe Him, or we don't. Actions follow belief.

"And it shall come to pass, as soon as the soles of the feet of the priests that bear the ark of the Lord, *the Lord of all the earth,* [that's who is leading us] shall rest in the waters of the Jordan, that the waters of the Jordan shall be cut off from the waters that come down from above; and they shall stand upon an heap."

It happened. Some say the water stood 150 feet high.

The priests with the ark stood in the middle of the Jordan until every man, woman, child, and animal had passed over. While this was going on, God had one man from each of the twelve tribes pick up a stone from the riverbed and place it where the ark had stood. Then each man went back and got another stone and carried it out to the bank of the river to make a monument there.

Why?

These were to be memory stones. The pile in the midst of the river would be covered when the water came crashing down to its place. To me this is symbolic of the personal, private memories we all have of the times God has intervened in the depths of our lives, the things we keep hidden.

The other cairn Joshua and the Israelites were to build was to be on the Jericho side of the river for everyone to see, but especially for the children. "When your children shall ask their fathers in time to come, saying, "What mean these stones?' then you shall let your children know saying, 'Israel came over this Jordan on dry land.' " God held back the waters of the Jordan for this generation, just as He had the waters of the Red Sea for their fathers, "That all the people of the earth might know the hand of the Lord, that it is mighty, that ye might fear the Lord your God forever."

In the years since our fire, we have had many

deep places in which to lay down memory stones, memorials to God's goodness to us. This book is my cairn on the bank, where everyone can see what God has done for me.

Danny was finally brought back to us — he had been away nine months — and from working in a machine shop in Forestville, where the fire occurred, Lloyd became a life insurance agent with the John Hancock Company in Buffalo. Then my health moved us to Dallas with the same company. After moving into a beautiful new home there, I was burning leftover cardboard boxes one day when a capricious wind flew a flaming box against my bad leg. I couldn't move without falling into the fire. I yelled, and Pete and Dan came running and knocked the burning piece back into the fire and helped me into the house. It was quite a burn. That happened in 1951. In 1978, surgery to wire up my fallen right arch also included extension of the Achilles tendon to improve mobility. The incision was made in the very spot where the burn had occurred. When the cast came off three months later, there was a necrotic ulcer four inches long, an inch wide, all the way in to the bone. Apparently the earlier burn had killed the nerve ends and, feeling no pain from the ulcer, I had no way of knowing how acute it had become.

Three months of soaking the foot three times a day in phisohex and sterile water were required to build up the muscle tissue to the point where the skin graft could be applied. I was teaching by that time, and by using a wheel chair I could keep pressure off the leg so that it was ready for a skin graft by Christmas vacation.

Knowing that I'd be spending two weeks immobilized so the graft would take, I researched fox squirrels. My first children's book, *Danger Comes to Squirrel Valley*, was published by Moody Press in 1979. That memory stone took a long time to set in place.

While we lived in Dallas, God read our desire to be in Christian work, and He took away the high overhead of our new house and Lloyd became manager of Camp El Har, southwest of Dallas, where another memory stone was picked up.

The area boasted the presence of four venomous snakes of the Southwest, and I was forced to turn the children over to the Lord daily. Worry is unbelief. When I came right down to it, I realized it was stupid to think that if the children were within sight, I could control their safety. In one day we saw all four kinds of snakes.

Lloyd had an early morning rendevous with a copperhead that was wound around the pump head. He bludgeoned it to an untimely death, at the same time putting the water system out of commission. At noon Pete uncovered a water moccasin a few inches from his hand as he lowered ice into the water fountain cooler. At about 5 P.M. as we were leaving camp, a coral snake crossed the road in front of us. The boys weren't able to catch it. That evening, back in camp, Suzy and our secretary, Ruth, trailed their bathrobes over a hid-

den diamond-backed rattler and woke him so he
was poised and rattling when Pete and Danny
almost stepped into him. Life was one day at a
time. What I usually forget is that life is always one
day at a time. God gives us grace for the day, not
for next week.

When Pete was in the eighth grade and Lloyd
took him to the Carroll Clinic for a routine pre-foot-
ball checkup, Pete's world tumbled around his
ears. The doctor said afterward, "All I can say is
that someone must have been sitting on my
shoulder to cause me to take X-rays of a perfectly
healthy boy." He found a vertebra in the lower back
almost *out* of the spinal column. The fact that no
pain had yet been felt made medical history. Dr.
Barnes used the X-rays in medical meetings for a
year proving his point that the slippage preceded
the pain, an idea new to many doctors. Pete's problem had been caused by a congenital defect: That
vertebra had no spur to hold it in place in the
column.

"What ifs" stupefied us. The two weeks immediately before, Pete had spent at Brigade Camp in
Tennessee, and he had helped carry a canoe over
several portages. What if his back had been strained too much in that trip? At El Har he had carried
fifty pounds of ice and many cases of pop as he
managed the camp store. What if...? But the big-
gest was what if he'd started football without that
particular checkup? One scrimmage, and he could
have died or been permanently crippled from the
waist down. Only the grace of God protected him

from the *what ifs*. It took two years for proper bone growth to permit him to play football, but he did play, and captained his team in his senior year.

The "all things" comprehension has ruled our lives and brought peace and comfort in the deepest water, the water where we have planted memory stones.

Moving from Dallas to Sky Ranches, Inc., a non-demoninational camp, was a faith-filled exercise. Lloyd worked in a hardware store; I served as a doctor's receptionist.

But I needed to be free in the summer to be with the children. That's when I started teaching. I began with eighth grade English in Duncanville. Lloyd finished work on his undergraduate degree at North Texas University and taught fifth grade, acting as principal of fifth and sixth grades.

When Sky Ranches purchased land up near Denton, we transferred, teaching in Lewisville and managing the camp in the summertime. And it was time for another memory stone.

In 1961, while we were in Lewisville, mononucleosis laid me down. Daddy and Mother sent me an airplane ticket so I could enjoy my convalescence in Hamburg with them instead of being at home alone with everyone else in school. What warm, wonderful fellowship we had! I was the only one of the children who hadn't seen Mother and Daddy in two years. Still Chief Engineer of Trico Products in Buffalo at age 75, Daddy was a vibrant, active man. On Thursday of that week as he and one of his fellow engineers were returning to Trico after lunch. He stepped up onto the curb in front of the Buffalo *Evening News* building, and fell dead.

As always, God's timing for me had been perfect. He had brought me home and given me time with my parents in the middle of the school year—an impossibility for a teacher! No, a grace gift for which I shall always be thankful. The "all things" were so evidently working together for my comfort that I couldn't miss the message.

As the memory stones went down in tough places, we learned to apply 1 Peter 5:7 time and time again. We dumped our irritations, our frustrations, our headaches, our backaches, our heartaches, and my falls on God. We know that when we did, they became His responsibilities. It seemed we kept having to learn this over and over.

Each of my frequent trips to the hospital has given us a chance to trust the Lord again. Every time I go, I pray, "Lord, please open my eyes to the things You want me to do here. Don't let me mess it up or miss any opportunity. This is Your party."

Someone has said, "How much so ever we have to do of business, we must not omit what we have to do for the glory of God, for that is our best business."

An accident at Sky Ranch sliced my chin open several inches and made one occasion apparently designed by God for me to praise Him in the hospital. A young woman reevaluated her relationship to Him to the glory of God.

Another time, ten days in Good Samaritan Hospital in Phoenix for intravenous gantrimycin to stamp out pseudomodas in my lungs took the life-giving information to my roommate that brought her into a positive relationship with the Lord that will last for eternity. How grateful I am for the grace of God!

In 40 years of life together, Lloyd and I have moved 33 times. That includes military moves, sometimes several a year. We have lived in new houses, in a tent, in a garage of friends, in two little trailers, in a big double-wide, in mansions and in cottages.

After the military, when the moves were our own decision, we learned that if God wanted us to move, or to get the job, then nothing could stand in the way. If He didn't want us to have it, we didn't want it. Being out of the will of God sets up real fear within us.

With every move to a different locale, we found marvelous fellowship with other believers. It's great to meet the people we'll live with throughout eternity. Paul encapsulates the experience when he says: "Eye hath not seen, nor ear heard, neither have entered into the heart of man the things which God hath prepared for them that love Him. But God hath revealed them unto us by his Spirit."[1] People outside of the royal family of God don't have the faintest idea of the joys of Christian fellowship.

And they don't have any idea of the blessings that can come from altars built by the memory stones God causes us to lay down.

# CHAPTER
## TEN

## Four-Point Plan

The years have presented a kaleidoscope of experiences: comfortable times, exciting situations, difficult learning periods, disappointing occurrences.

Although good news is magically energizing, lifting the heart, causing the spirit to soar, as I look back, the things I remember are the hard times: the enforced rests when God met me in the dark, the disappointments that threw my weight on Him, the painful happenings that stretched me, educated me, brought growth.

In the good times, in the excitement, I am thankful. But I coast; I don't grow. So, "Lest I should be exalted above measure...there was given to me a thorn in the flesh...Most gladly therefore will I rather glory in my infirmities, that the power of Christ may rest upon me....for when I am weak, then I am strong."[1] As I have turned my dreams over to God, their fulfillment is no longer as important to me.

An early growing experience came about some time after the fire. Lloyd had moved his two little boys and his crippled, pregnant wife into the only house available near Hamburg and Buffalo, a summer cottage on Lake Erie.

Then, on November 24, 1945, a Caesarian section brought us our third boy. We named him Theodore (Dorothy backwards), meaning "gift of

God." Lloyd brought us home on a toboggan, leaving the car on the highway. Even for Buffalo it was the "year of the BIG SNOW."

My frustration was that I wanted a girl! Surely God knew that. He did. He also knew we needed Ted. We piled the problem on God; it was His. Within two years this very pressure made a home for a little girl, Susan Jo, who had no father and whose mother had just undergone a radical mastectomy and had little assurance of much of a future.

At this point my frustration at being denied a girl transferred to the irritation of having one, and the heartache of viewing the scars with which multi-rejection had disfigured her soul. Physically her problems responded to treatment, but her fears were unfathomable. Her needs kept me on my knees. Only God could provide solutions.

As the children grew older, other frustrations transformed themselves into a program of training. With legs that worked only when I stacked one bone on top of another before transferring my weight from the previously stacked set, I was severely limited in what I could do for my family. The chores of housecleaning, getting meals, cleaning up after themselves, shopping, and almost everything else, fell within the children's province. As a result, all four of the kids have become accomplishers of superior caliber. God knew what was best. In denying me He built them.

Possibly the hardest, longest lasting, and most frequent learning experiences for all of us were my falls.

The doctor had told me, "You will never be able to take a step without first checking the floor with your eyes to locate a piece of lettuce, a slippery spot, an obstruction that will upset your equilibrium. Never." He was right. When I didn't do just that, I fell as a pan would drop.

Sometimes I fell forward on my knees. The weak right side always went down first and hardest and the right knee swelled to double its normal size more than once. On one occasion the doctor said he would have to aspirate it because it would not reduce. I turned it over to the Lord. It was one of the "all things" that He was capable of utilizing for good. How, I couldn't guess.

The day before the dreaded aspiration, I tumbled again but only part way, catching myself on the corner of a couch. The fall was sufficient, though to snap the swollen leg back. *God* aspirated it, and before morning the knee was down to normal size.

As I think over the falls of 39 years, at least 500 of them, I am amazed. Lots of hurt, but no broken bones, with the exception of a fractured coccyx that my wise doctor X-rayed and set, instructing me to sit on a book with the tailbone hanging over the edge. I was teaching at Yavapai College then. I didn't miss a class.

At first the falls were from inexperience with both my inabilities and with the things that cause falls. In the hospital it was lack of concentration. Later, carelessness, hurrying, over confidence, and unseen humps or snags figured in my downfalls. Sometimes I'd be going about my business, being a good girl, and the floor would just come up to greet me. On the other hand, I once climbed up on tables and wallpapered a wall (while Lloyd was gone) and had no problem.

Knowing this was to be a way of life, I had to adopt a philosophy that would glorify the Lord. What came about was total thankfulness. I could not fall if I were not walking. Every time I went down, I said, "Thank You, Lord!" And I meant it.

I came to realize that not having legs that work is like not having money. I'm limited in what I can do, but it's not the end of the world. Being deprived in one facet of my being forces me to develop others. (Lloyd says I have too many facets and they're always all turned on.) As a gardener, I know that if I want the bell peppers to produce heavily, I nip off the top bud. This forces it to push blossoms and fruit out from every other branch. Physical education was my top bud when I was in college. I dreamed of playing games with my children, of tramping through the woods with them, of skiing, skating, running with them. God nipped off my top bud. Pushed to sitting occupations, today I paint and write.

Now that the legs are really gone, I walk only with my "pogo sticks," quad canes that support my arms. I can't take a step without them. I don't fall as often, but when I do fall my arms come out bloody with great chunks of skin hanging. Kicking against the pricks is painful and counterproductive. What I can do, I shall do. What I can't, I won't weep over.

Learning through pain continues. Fifty years of living with the Lord have passed since that night in a Wheaton prayer meeting, and I have learned much about God and His way with His children when tragedy comes. I am indebted to Bob Thieme for providing me a Four-Point-Plan for Disaster. This plan helps me keep a divine perspective, a God-oriented attitude toward difficulties of any size, and the plan becomes my constant companion. Here is a "how-to" you don't want to underestimate:

Point One: *And we know that all things work together for good to them that love God, to them who are the called according to His purpose* (Romans 8:28). This has to be believed, or the other three points won't work.

When I *know* that whatever catastrophe presently engulfing me has been worked by God into His plan for my life—for eternal good—I can rest. I know that nothing can touch me unless He has permitted it; therefore, even though it is a toughie, He is with me, I can learn what He has for me to learn, and He has a *reason* for the assignment, or this thing wouldn't be happening. I can respond to Christ and not to the problem or the person because I know God's thoughts toward me are thoughts of peace and not of evil, to give me an expected end. (Jeremiah 29:11).

We have no control over our circumstances, but God has. However, we make our own mental and spiritual environment. We must believe Him and trust Him; there is no other option for His children.

Point Two: *Let Him have all your worries and*

*cares, for He is always thinking about you and watching everything that concerns you* (I Peter 5:7, TLB).

God never intended for His children to carry their burdens, their problems, their difficulties. Jesus Christ is prepared to do it. He wants to do it. However, He will let us carry them if we prefer. He's a gentleman; he won't interfere. He will never put His finger into our heads and press the *yes* button. It grieves Him to see us bent under a load that He is waiting to carry.

He watches everything that concerns us. And he does his watching from the vantage point of His seat at the right hand of God the Father. He "makes intercession for us" there (Romans 8:34).

At this point, when I agree that God is able to mesh this horrible thing (even my dumb mistakes) into the eternal gears for good, and I unload it on Him, I can be thankful for it. I can keep reminding myself that it is His problem, not mine any more. With every difficulty I am privileged to view one more instance where He moves in power.

That is Point Three: *In everything give thanks, for this is the will of God in Christ Jesus concerning you.* (I Thessalonians 5:18). If that doesn't nail it down for you, try Ephesians 5:20: *Giving thanks always for all things unto God and the Father in the name of our Lord Jesus Christ.*

Thankfulness is a catalyst. It changes the chemistry of the attitude. I am not to be thankful that it isn't any worse, or that the hurt will soon be over; I'm to be thankful for the pain, for the problem, for the disaster. Why? For one thing, it brings me closer to the Lord. Where does He want me? Close. Near. Depending on Him. For another thing it indicates trust. I *know* I can trust Him to have my best interests at heart. Romans 5 says if God did the most for us when we were His enemies, what will He do for us now that we are His children? Answer: More than that most. My insides smooth out when I think about that, and I am thankful. I have peace. With that attitude, with the Lord carrying the misery, I can relax.

The last point is the frosting on the cake. Point Four: *The battle is the Lord's* (I Samuel 117:47b). I don't have to fight the battle; it's not mine to fight. It's God's. Like Moses, I can "stand still and see the deliverance of the Lord." Exodus 14:13 and the following verse, "The Lord shall fight for you and you shall hold your peace." II Chronicles 20:15 and 17: "Thus saith the Lord unto you, 'Be not afraid nor dismayed by reason of this great multitude; for the battle is not yours, but God's...You shall not need to fight in this battle: set yourselves, stand still, and see the salvation of the Lord with you'."

When people ask me how I feel these days, I can always say, "Great!" My soul is at peace, my spirit is in fellowship, and it's only the body that hurts so two-thirds of me is great, and that's a majority. On the inside, as Joyce Landorf's little granddaughter says, "I can sing and dance."

What a glorious place to be!

We're on the winning side of the Great Battle. We know the outcome. Praise God that He permits us to witness, even take part in a few of the skirmishes.

When we let God write the ticket, the program, the plan for our lives, His purposes are fulfilled. His blueprint is engaged. He is glorified, and so are we. Romans 8:30.

# NOTES

**Chapter 1**
1. C.S. Lewis, *The Problem of Pain*. New York: MacMillan, 1971, p. 93.

**Chapter 2**
1. Matthew 11:28-30

**Chapter 3**
1. Job 1:21
2. Psalm 119:11
3. John 14:26
4. C.S. Lewis, *The Problem of Pain*. New York: MacMillan, 1971.

**Chapter 4**
1. C.S. Lewis, *The Problem of Pain* New York: Mac Millan, 1971, p. 95.
2. Thomas Aquinas

**Chapter 5**
1. Deuteronomy 33:25
2. 1 Samuel 8:4-22

**Chapter 6**
1. Psalm 127:2

**Chapter 8**
1. Deuteronomy 8:3

**Chapter 9**
1. 1 Corinthians 2:9,10

**Chapter 10**
1. 2 Corinthians 12:7-10